IMAGES
of America

CANTON

THE FONTAINE SISTERS, C. LATE 1920S. Doris Danis (1909–1978), pictured on the left, danced for ten years with her partner, Sunny O'Dea. En route to Hollywood, she was persuaded by the love of her life, Leo Abramowitz (1910–1986), to forgo her dancing career and return with him to Canton, where they were wed on August 21, 1937. (Courtesy of Marilyn Abramowitz.)

IMAGES
of America

CANTON

R. Marc Kantrowitz

ARCADIA
PUBLISHING

ISBN 978-1-5316-0270-3

Published by Arcadia Publishing
Charleston, South Carolina

Library of Congress Catalog Card Number: 00-104071

For all general information contact Arcadia Publishing at:
Telephone 843-853-2070
Fax 843-853-0044
E-mail sales@arcadiapublishing.com
For customer service and orders:
Toll-Free 1-888-313-2665

Visit us on the Internet at www.arcadiapublishing.com

On the cover: CANTON HIGH SCHOOL BASEBALL TEAM, C. EARLY 1930S. Pictured in front of Canton's second high school, the Hemenway, the team's first string appears to be featured in the front row. Today, the high school building is used for elderly housing.

Dedicated to the people of Canton, past and present, who have made this town what it is today. Only through the continuing unselfish devotion of those fortunate enough to reside here will the town continue to prosper and flourish.

A HOUSE ON THE GO, 1956. With the construction of Interstate 93, houses had to be demolished or relocated. Saved from the wrecking ball, this lovely home was moved. The Blue Hills are seen in the background. (Courtesy of the Gibbs Family.)

CONTENTS

Acknowledgments

At the outset, it is important to state what this book is and what it is not. This volume is not a comprehensive overview of the town of Canton, rather it is picture driven. Accordingly, if an adequate picture of, say, a school or church could not be obtained, that school or church was not included.

Pictures were gathered, as Blanche DuBois might observe, through the kindness of strangers. My chore was made far easier through the goodwill, enthusiasm, and generosity of some whose assistance went far and above the call. They came to the aid of one they did not know; most notably are Chris Brindley, Joe DeFelice, Ann Galvin, Jean Galvin, Mark Lague of the Canton Public Library, Blanche Danahy Nervi, and Peg Morse Wentworth.

In no particular order, I wish to thank the many other people who helped me in the writing of this book: Bill and Patrick Galvin; Ed Galvin; Ann Leonard Brindley; Ed Bolster; Ed Lynch; Dan Keleher; Sheila Simms; Mona Podgurski; Velma Coffey; Peter Sarra; Glen Hannington, Esq.; John Galvin, Esq.; Mark and Sue Gibbs; Joe and Maryann Kinnealey; Dr. and Mrs. John Crowe; Police Chief Peter Bright; Fr. John McCune of St. John's Church; Cynthia McDonough; Donald Wheeler; Beverly Beckham; Selectman John Connelly; Mr. and Mrs. Charles Tolias; Paul Rogers; Beverly Foley, CAI; Melinda and John McLaughlin; Dave and Joe Masciarelli; Marie and Alan Leary; Bob Barbaglia; Mark, Stan, and Marylou Parrish; Father McLaughlin, St. Gerard's Church; Briget Meehan; Chrissy Smith; Kay Gleason of Historical Inc. (www.oldmapsne.com); Patti Ryburn; David Mann; Al D'Attanasio; Ed Maguire; Mary Walkup; Al and Marie Leary; Jim Roache; Rick Saquet; Dan Erickson; Beth Erickson and Mary Ann Price, *Canton Citizen*; Dennis Tatz and David Connolly, *Patriot Ledger*; Christina Wallace; Bill Thibeault; Marilyn Abramowitz; the Cohen family; Anthony Mitchell Sammarco; Don Rittner; Amy Sutton, my editor at Arcadia; the Archdiocese of Boston; Amanda Slater; Bill Sweeney; Debbie Sullivan, Franchise Associates Inc.; Bill Burdick, the Baseball Hall of Fame; Secretary of State William Francis Galvin; Michael Comeau, Archives Department, secretary of state's office; Jeff Curran; Marilyn Curran; Ralph Staples; and, saving the best for last, my family, Marianne Larson and Matthew and Sara Kantrowitz. If I have failed to include someone, please accept my sincere apologies.

Bibliography and Research Information

Burke, Gerard F. *Canton, 1979–1947.* Town of Canton, 1947.

Centennial of St. John the Evangelist Parish, 1861–1961. St. John's, 1961.

Erickson, Dan. *Paul Revere's Life in Canton, Massachusetts.* Senior History Project, 1993.

Galvin, Edward D. *A History of Canton Junction.* Sculpin Publications, 1987.

Huntoon, Daniel T.V. *History of Canton, Mass.* Cambridge: John Wilson and Son. University Press, 1893.

Lynch, Ed, Dan Keleher, Ed Bolster, Chris Brindley, Jim Roache, Peter Pineo. *Canton Comes of Age, 1797–1997.* Published by the Town of Canton, 1997.

Reynolds, Alice. *Who Was Who and What Was What in the History of Canton, Mass.* Friends of the Little Red House Inc., 1975.

Other sources include the Canton Public Library; the *Canton Citizen*; the *Canton Journal*; Canton High School yearbooks; and interviews with Canton residents.

While every effort has been made to identify those pictured, mistakes are inevitable. Please forgive and correct any errors so that future editions may be updated.

INTRODUCTION

Canton may have gotten off on the wrong foot. Not only did Stoughton not wish us to remain part of their town, but our name was derived due to the mistaken belief that if one drilled straight through the earth from Canton, Massachusetts, that Canton, China, would be the ultimate destination. Perhaps if our forefathers were geographically more sophisticated in 1797, we would have been called, as some proposed at the time, Duxbury or Ponkapoag.

Despite the shaky "official" start of the town in 1797, our heritage actually predates the founding by nearly 150 years. As far back as 1650, the Ponkapoag area, which included what is now Canton, was settled. If Canton had a grandmother, Dorchester would have been her name. Dorchester, which in the 1600s was New England's largest town, gave birth to Milton (1662), Wrentham (1724), Foxborough (1778), and Stoughton (1726). Stoughton included what ultimately would become Canton (1797) and Sharon (1765).

Needless to say, the Native Americans had a great presence in the area; indeed, the land was originally all theirs. When our forefathers landed at Plymouth in 1620, the Indian tribe called Massachusetts, under their great Chief Chicataubut, was in possession of the land. The Massachusetts Indians who settled in the Neponset River area were called the Neponset Indians. It was that tribe—whose chief was Kitchamakin, Chicataubut's successor—to whom the Great Apostle John Eliot first preached in 1646.

The name of the territory beyond the Blue Hills was Ponkapoag and when some of the Native American tribe migrated there, they became known as the Ponkapoag Indians. Interestingly, as Canton's greatest historian Daniel Huntoon (p. 126) observed, it was the Native Americans who took the name of the land rather than the other way around.

One of the great Native American families were the Ahautons. Old Ahauton's son, William (also known as Quaanan), was to sign many deeds and documents and did much of the negotiating between the parties living in the area. Ahauton died in 1711. His wigwam was where Canton High School stands today.

One of the earliest settlers in Canton was John Wentworth, who left Maine between 1690 and 1700 after encountering some troubles with the Native Americans living there. To this date, the Wentworth family owns a house in Canton on Washington Street and have added much to the town. Larra Edwin Wentworth (1844–1912) fought in the Civil War (pp. 26–28) while Nathaniel Newcomb Wentworth Jr. (1917–1992) (pp. 33, 123) saw action in World War II.

Canton's first minister was Joseph Morse (1671–1732) of the First Congregational Church. He graduated Harvard in 1695 and was installed here in 1717. He lasted approximately ten years and left under a cloud of controversy, some alleging him to "false speaking, criminal lying," and drinking. Whether these charges were true or not could not be discerned when Huntoon examined the issue in 1893, although Huntoon opined Morse to be amicable, scholarly, and meek, who shrunk and retreated from the conflict rather than stay and fight.

The oldest road in Canton is Washington Street, which runs from Cobb's Corner (where Canton, Sharon, and Stoughton meet) through downtown Canton, past the high school, cemeteries, making a left at the Ponkapoag Golf Course (and becoming Route 138 in the process), and going all the way past the Blue Hills to the Milton line. Sections of the road were in existence in the mid-1600s. Over the years, it was called a variety of names—including the King's Highway, the Country Road, the Main Road Leading to Rhode Island, Taunton Road, the Great Road from Boston to Taunton, and the Main Road—before finally being given its current name, Washington Street, in 1840. Not only were the names different over the years, but so was the shape of the road and where it traveled. Its latest, most significant change came in the 1950s, when Route 93 was built, although it has changed recently to accommodate Reebok coming to town.

When formal education first arrived in 1726, lessons were taught in the home of Robert Redman. It was not until 1760 that Canton saw its first schoolhouse located in Ponkapoag. In 1771, this schoolhouse was replaced by one located near St. Mary's Cemetery. The small red building existed until 1809. Over the next century, schoolhouses came and went, located in all different areas of town. Today, some are still in existence, used in a variety of ways—the Gridley (a preschool, p. 63), Revere Street (a gardening-landscaping business, p. 56), and Pleasant Street (a private home) to name but a few. Today, Canton has three public elementary schools—the Luce (p. 73), Kennedy, and Hanson, one middle school (the Galvin), and one high school (Canton High School, p. 52). There are other schools in town including the Massachusetts Hospital School (p. 66) for physically challenged children and the Blue Hills Technical School, which teaches trades to high school students. There were two high schools prior to the present one (pp. 50, 52).

To gain a true sense of the history of old Canton, one need not go any further than a walk through one of its several graveyards. The oldest, located on Washington Street, is called the "Oldest Burying Ground, 1700" (p. 79). The town cemetery is located across from St. Mary's Cemetery. The short tales engraved on ancient gravestones tell centuries-old stories of the death of a civil war soldier (p. 30) or the tragic early demise of a young child (p. 18). Some are lyrical, others stark. The gravestone of Jesse Wentworth reads, "Mourn not for me; / Death is a debt / To nature due, / That I have paid, / And so must you." The tomb of William Glover reads, "My Loving Friends, as you pass by, / On my cold grave, pray cast your eye. / Your sun, like mine, may set at noon, / Your soul be called for very soon."

Over the years, Canton has had its share of well-known and influential people. Paul Revere (pp. 118–119) lived and worked here and made Canton the nation's leading copper manufacturing center for a rather lengthy period. Gen. Richard Gridley, a Revolutionary War hero, started the U.S. Army Corps of Engineers. Comm. John Downes was a great navel hero during our war for independence. Roger Sherman, who grew up in Canton, signed and wrote, along with John Adams, Thomas Jefferson, Benjamin Franklin, and Robert Livingston, the Declaration of Independence. Sherman, who relocated to Connecticut, was a treasurer at Yale, a Superior Court judge, and a U.S. senator in the First Congress.

An industrial superweight, Canton has been a manufacturing leader for over two centuries. Whether it was Revere's copper, Drapers's Woolens Goods (p. 23), Elijah Morse's Rising Sun Company (pp. 120–121), or the production of artificial skin today for burn victims, Canton has held a noteworthy position.

In sports, whenever one watches a professional baseball game, it seems that Bobby Witt's first name is Canton's Own. However, long before Witt, Canton's Own Olaf Henrikson (pp. 117, 128) was a 1912 World Series hero. Other sports leaders, past and present, include Mark Sullivan and Luis Tiant (Boston Red Sox) and Steve Rooney (Montreal Canadians) to name but a few.

To learn more about the legacy of Canton, visit its historical society and library and speak with today's town historians (pp. 126–128), who have helped keep the past alive. Lastly, there is a wealth of written information, much of it listed in the bibliography; learn of the paths our predecessors walked, taking the same steps on the same land, decades and even centuries later.

One

CANTON THROUGH
THE YEARS

CHARLIE GRIMES'S STABLE, C. 1895. This photograph shows Charlie Grimes sitting in his carriage outside of his stable on Washington Street, across from St. John's Church. Charlie ran a livery, hack, and boarding stable on that site from 1892 until it burned down in 1917. At one time, Charlie owned every house on Ames Avenue; he built a new house at 36 Ames Avenue for his family in 1915. (Courtesy of Edward D. Galvin.)

THE IRONWORKS. Joseph H. Hidley, a painter of towns and religious subjects, was born in 1830 and died 42 years later. While he concentrated on towns located in New York, he ventured outside of his native state, as shown by this picture. This view of downtown Canton portrays a time and area far removed from the hustle and bustle of downtown Canton today. (Courtesy of Canton Public Library.)

THE OLD FENNO HOUSE. John Fenno Jr. may have moved to Canton as early as 1695. His two-story house, built in 1704, was a rarity in those days and is probably a strong indicator of his apparent wealth. He married Rachel Newcom c. 1690 and died on April 23, 1741 at the age of 76. His house was moved from Canton and is now located in Sturbridge Village. (Courtesy of Joe DeFelice.)

THE DAVENPORT HOUSE. The Jonathan Puffer house in Ponkapoag was built in 1711. The house is more commonly known as the John Davenport house. John purchased the house from Jonathan Puffer in 1717, and it remained under Davenport ownership for 183 years. It is rumored that the Ponkapoag Indians helped to build the house, which was not an unusual practice. This house is believed to be the oldest home in Canton since the Fenno house (1704) was moved to Sturbridge Village in 1949. However, a portion of the "Little Red House" at Pequitside farm may predate the Puffer House by at least ten years. (Courtesy of Canton Public Library.)

11

THE TILDEN HOUSE. The Little Red House, as it is commonly known today, at Pequitside Farm is more properly referred to as the David Tilden House. Tilden bought the house and land from Native Americans in 1725. The plan of the land showed an existing two-story structure already on the property. It is known that Jabez Searle died here in 1724. Probably the most noted owner was Rev. Zachariah Howard and his wife, Martha, commonly known as Polly. This house is owned by the Town of Canton. It is in serious disrepair and in jeopardy of being demolished. (Courtesy of Canton Public Library.)

THE CRANE HOUSE. The Crane House on Green Street, commonly referred to as the Nathan Crane House, more accurately should be called the Deacon Eliu Crane House. The house was built the same year that Nathan was born, 1748. Militia Gen. Nathan Crane saw some service in the Revolutionary Army and was active in town affairs. Nathan was known as the "Northern General" as not to confuse him with Gen. Elijah Crane from South Canton. Their political views were as far apart as their residences. (Courtesy of Canton Public Library.)

12

CARROLL'S TAVERN. St. Gerard's Church now stands where Carroll's Tavern once stood on Washington Street. Erected on April 4, 1798, the tavern was kept by Samuel Carroll, who married a daughter of Adam Blackman. It was in the hall of this tavern that the first Baptist minister preached on September 4, 1806. Also in 1806, meetings were held here to oppose the building of the turnpike. Samuel Carroll died on October 25, 1820. (Courtesy of Canton Public Library.)

THE ENDICOTT HOUSE. The James Endicott House at 1044 Washington was completed early in 1807. The original house that stood there was build c. 1710 and burned down on October 29, 1806. The house burned rapidly because the militia's gunpowder was stored in the basement. In 1809, a powderhouse was built behind Pequitside Farm. This was the first brick building in Canton; the town hall was the third. James Endicott was born in 1766 and for many years was a school teacher. He was prominent in town affairs. He died on February 22, 1834. A recent addition to the home nearly matches the original structure. (Courtesy of Canton Public Library.)

THE OLD TOWN HOUSE. This structure was built by the Baptist Society in 1819 as a meetinghouse at the cost of $2,000. In 1826, the town purchased and used it for town purposes until 1879, when it was closed. Canton's first town meeting was held here in 1824. Sold at auction, it was taken down in 1884. This picture was taken from the Town of Canton Annual Report of 1885. The historical blurb accompanying the picture was written by none other than Daniel Huntoon, Canton's greatest historian. (Courtesy of Peg Wentworth Morse.)

THE OLD MANSE HOUSE. "The Old Parsonage," in which three generations of Dunbars lived, was torn down in 1884. The land on which the house stood was purchased by John Withington from the Ponkapoag Indians. In 1728, he sold the property to Samuel Dunbar (p. 78), who built a large and lovely residence, thought to be one of the most beautiful in the area. Ultimately, the Drapers built a large Victorian structure, which currently stands at 87 Chapman Street. (Courtesy of Canton Public Library.)

THE OLD INGRAHAM SCHOOL. Like many buildings, this one also had a long and varied history. Erected in 1827 at Ingraham's Corner near Washington and Neponset Streets, it was built of stone at the request of Gen. Elijah Crane, who agreed to pay the difference between the cost of a wooden and stone house. At one point, it served as a schoolhouse. In 1836, it was converted into a store, owned at different times by Amos Holmes, C. Dennison, and the Fuller Brothers. (Courtesy of Canton Public Library.)

THE OLD POOR FARM. In 1885, the town elected to spend $10,000 to construct this building for the town's less fortunate. Located on Walpole Street, it replaced the dilapidated one on Pleasant Street. Designed by noted local architect George Walter Capen, the house was completed in 1888. (Courtesy of Canton Public Library.)

I have written my sister in such a way that she will be almost sure to come to our wedding. I have promised to send my mother $500 — in a short time — & I will pay my sister's expenses too.

I talked last night in Canton, & had the hospitalities of Mr. Ames (son of Oakes Ames the P.R.R. Mogul) inflicted on me — & it is the last time I will stop in a New England private house. Their idea of hospitality is to make _themselves_ comfortable _first_, & leave the guest to get along _if he can_. No _smoking_ allowed _on the premises_. The next New Englander that receives me into his house will take me as I _am_, not as I ought to be. To curtail a guest's liberties & demand that he shall come up to the host's peculiar self-righteous ideas of virtue, is simply pitiful & contemptible. I hate Mr. Ames with all my heart. I had no sleep last night & must seek some rest, little sweetheart. Bless you my own darling, whom I love better & better & more & more tenderly every day.

Sam.

A Letter from Mark Twain, December 21, 1869, from Canton. Samuel Langhorne Clemens, more commonly known as Mark Twain, was born on November 30, 1835 and died April 21, 1910. He once visited Canton. As his letter indicates (written to his fiancee Olivia Langdon of Elmira, New York), his stay here was not quite up to his standards. At the time, Twain was in the Boston area from November 10, 1869 to January 26, 1870, perhaps speaking on his new book *Innocence Abroad*. His wedding was planned for Christmas or New Year's Eve, but due to his speaking tour, he did not get married until February 2, 1870. (Courtesy of the Mark Twain Papers, the Bancroft Library, University of California, Berkeley; the text is copyright 1949 by the Mark Twain Foundation.)

THE WENTWORTH FARM, C. 1876. This lovely farm was located just outside of downtown Canton heading toward Cobb's Corner. The Wentworth family goes back generations and still maintains a presence in modern-day Canton. It all started with Elder William Wentworth (1615–1696), whose son John settled in Canton between 1690 and 1700 from York, Maine, to escape a dispute with Native Americans. (Courtesy of Peg Wentworth Morse.)

THE WENTWORTH FARM, 40 YEARS LATER, 1916. The Wentworth garage was started in a barn on the property in 1910 by Nathaniel Newcomb Wentworth. It moved into the shop, pictured above on the left, which was built next to the barn in 1916. An addition to the rear of the garage expanded it in 1928. Wentworth Garage was renamed the Wentworth Motor Company, prior to its being sold in 1946. The buildings are still owned by the Wentworth family. Wentworth, who was born in 1884, died on November 9, 1952. (Courtesy of Peg Wentworth Morse.)

FATHER AND DAUGHTER. Larra Wentworth is pictured with his young daughter, Rebecca. This fetching child died on March 25, 1881, at the age of 14. While the cause of her death is not known, the loss caused great sadness in the Wentworth family. Father and daughter are buried in adjoining graves in the Canton Cemetery. (Courtesy of Peg Wentworth Morse.)

A PORTRAIT OF FAMILY AND FRIENDS. In the spring of 1893, Ada Dow memorialized 11 members of the Canton community, including some Wentworths, who were together celebrating an unspecified event. From the handwriting on the back of the picture, it is known that "Donald [stands] in front of Uncle Tom Dunbar, beside Aunt Louise." (Courtesy of Peg Wentworth Morse.)

A HORSE AND BUGGY ON ELM STREET, C. 1870s. The home at 35 Elm Street was built between 1839 and 1848. It was owned by the same family until 1963. At one time, Elm Street was called Back Street. One of its most illustrious residents was naval hero Comm. John Downes (1784–1854), to whom Daniel Huntoon devotes an entire chapter in his epic history book about Canton. (Courtesy Dr. John Crowe.)

FRENCH WALLPAPER. This elegant wallpaper was manufactured in France and hung in the house at 35 Elm Street in the mid-1800s, where it remained for over a century. Purchased by an antique dealer in the late 1950s, it was removed intact. Legend, perhaps apocryphal, has it that First Lady Jackie Kennedy was so taken by it that she had it purchased and hung in the Blair House in Washington. (Courtesy Dr. John Crowe)

19

A TROLLEY ON WASHINGTON STREET. The Blue Hill Street Railway made its last run in 1920, only two decades after it had opened. The winter of 1919–1920 was especially bad, stranding the trolley literally in its tracks. When the thaw finally came, it was too late to save the system, which died out due to the advent of the automobile, buses, and modern travel. (Courtesy of Rick Saquet.)

LIVINIA AND JOHN MCKENNA, C. LATE 1890s. Livinia Margaret McKenna, who was born in 1889, grew up, married, and became the mother of Edward Manning Cohen (p. 57). Her younger brother, John McKenna, is pictured to her left. Approximately 20 years after this photograph was taken, John died during the influenza epidemic. (Courtesy of the Cohen Family)

A LEISURELY DAY, 1916. What is known of these four people is that Elsie Wentworth is present, along with Herman, Charles, and Virginia. The house appears to be the Wentworth one located on Washington Street. (Courtesy of Peg Wentworth Morse.)

A TRAGIC FIRE, 1924. On Saturday, May 24, 1924, on the corner of Washington and Greenlodge Streets, fire consumed a two-family structure so quickly that, despite the best efforts of several onlookers, seven people died: Beatrice LeClaire (12), Rita LeClaire (8), twins Leo and Leona LeClaire (5), Antoinette D'Attanasio (33), Viola D'Attanasio (8), and Romano D'Attanasio. Pictured are Canton Police Chief John Flood and a fire marshall surveying the damage. (Courtesy of Al D'Attanasio.)

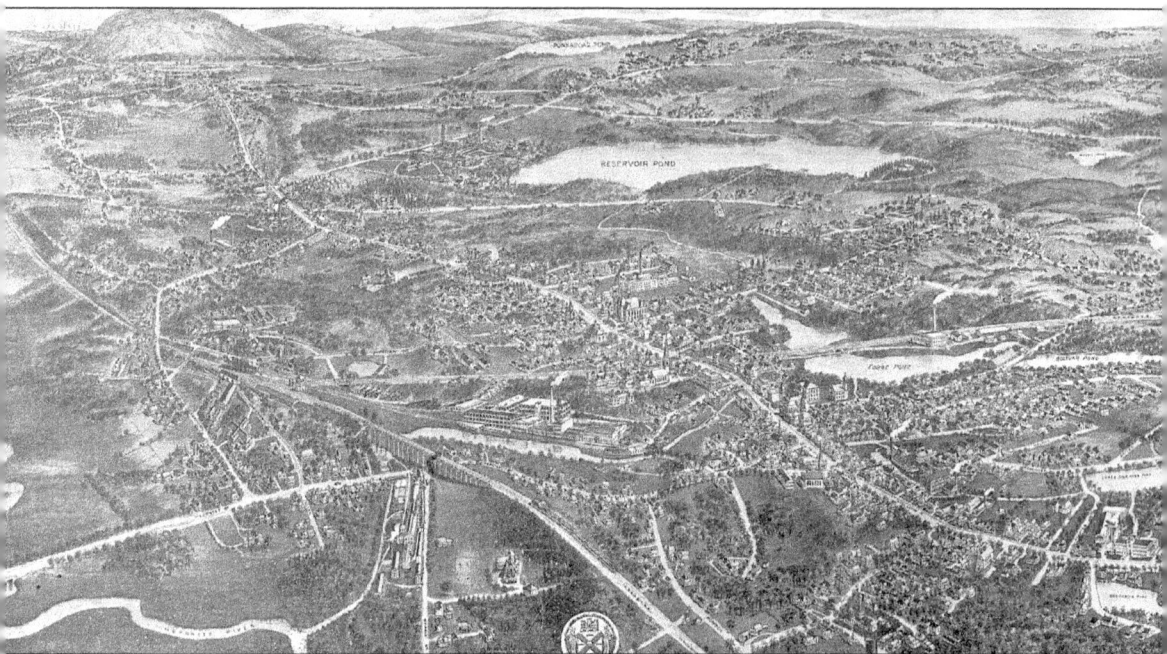

MAKE CANTON YOUR HOME!, C. 1917. This advertisement for the "attractive and prosperous Canton" details its many virtues, including the purity of its water, its low death rate, and its motorized fire department. (Courtesy of Canton Public Library.)

HOCKEY TEAM, C. 1940s. Hockey has been and continues to be a very popular sport in Canton. In the 1940s, it was played outside, frequently in an area called the Dogpatch. Located on Washington and Pecunit Streets, it was in the general vicinity of what is now the Hanson Elementary School. Today, the Dogpatch is filled in with dirt and overgrown brush, only a fond and distant memory to those old enough to remember it. (Courtesy of Al D'Attanasio.)

THE STORM OF 1944. The back of this picture tells the human side of a storm during the winter of 1944. Harry was stranded and could not get by Tobe's on Thursday night. He returned to the Washington Street site, off of Reynolds property, the next day to shovel out. (Courtesy of Chris Brindley.)

DRAPER WOOLENS'S PARADE FLOAT, 1947. Despite what the float indicates, the Drapers had been making woolen products even before 1856. Brothers Tom and James Draper brought the wool manufacturing business to Canton and through time saw it prosper, fail, change hands, relocate, and grow, all according to the economic climate at the time. In the 1850s, James Draper had a manufacturing plant on the property where the historical society stands today. (Courtesy of Canton Public Library.)

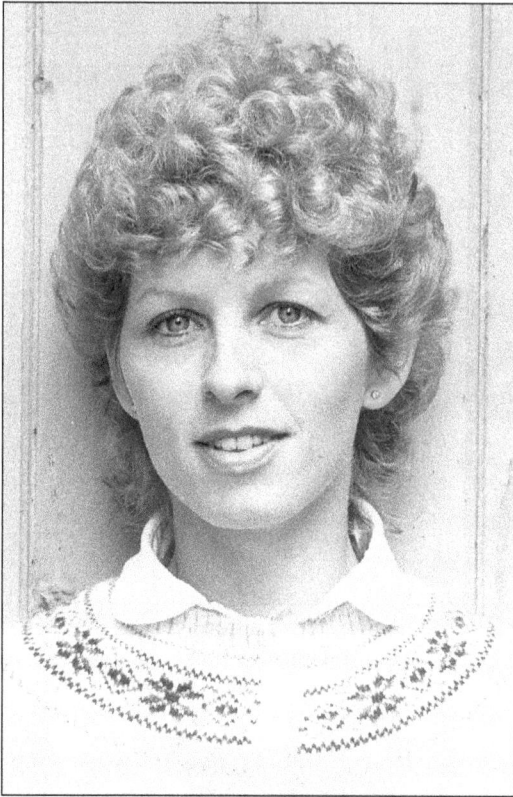

BEVERLY BECKHAM, C. LATE 1960S. Noted *Boston Herald* columnist and writer Beverly Beckham is a longtime Canton resident. Her latest book is *Back Then: A Memoir of Childhood*. Married for 32 years, she and her husband, Bruce, have three grown children. She is a frequent guest on television and radio and speaks throughout the nation on various topics. She started her career in 1979. (Courtesy of Beverly Beckham.)

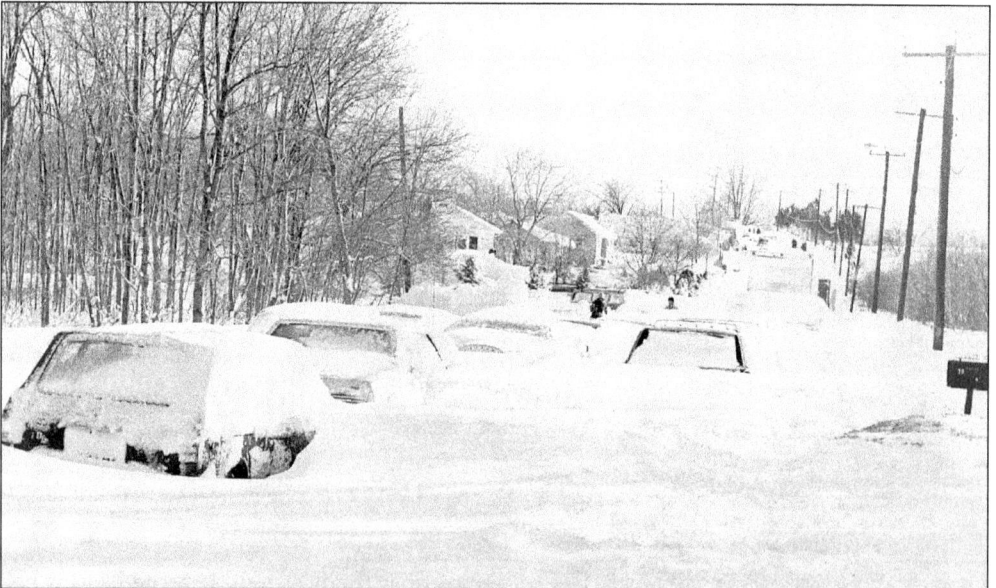

THE BLIZZARD OF 1978. This car graveyard of snow is typical of what many Canton residents experienced during one of the worst snowstorms of all time in the northeast. The Blizzard of 1978 affected an area far beyond Canton and the northeast. During the storm, scores of drivers found themselves stuck in their cars on impassable roads, forced to abandon their vehicles and make it home anyway they could. (Courtesy of Canton Public Library.)

Two

CANTON AT WAR

CIVIL WAR VETERANS. Judging from the appearance of these Civil War veterans, this photograph was probably taken in the late 1800s or early 1900s. Shown, from left to right, are Richard Weston, Theron Kelly, James Ryan, ? Stevens, a man identified only as the "York Street man," ? Priest, Owen Sullivan, ? Lentell, another "York Street man," and Charles Partridge. (Courtesy of Canton Public Library.)

LARRA EDWIN WENTWORTH IN 1862.
Larra Wentworth was born in 1844.
In 1862, he joined the Union Army.
This photograph shows how he looked
upon his induction. (Courtesy of Peg
Wentworth Morse.)

LARRA EDWIN WENTWORTH IN 1864.
One can see the effects of the Civil War
on Larra. This photograph, taken just two
years after his induction, shows a man
aged by the brutality of conflict. (Courtesy
of Peg Wentworth Morse.)

AN 1863 LETTER. This is the first page of a four-page letter, written on January 4, 1863, from Larra Wentworth, stationed in New York City, to his father in Canton. As the letter indicates, there are many men there from Massachusetts, serving in the same regiment. Shortly after this letter was written, Larra and his companions were sent to Louisiana, where they fought in a major campaign, the Battle of Fort Hudson. (Courtesy of Peg Wentworth Morse.)

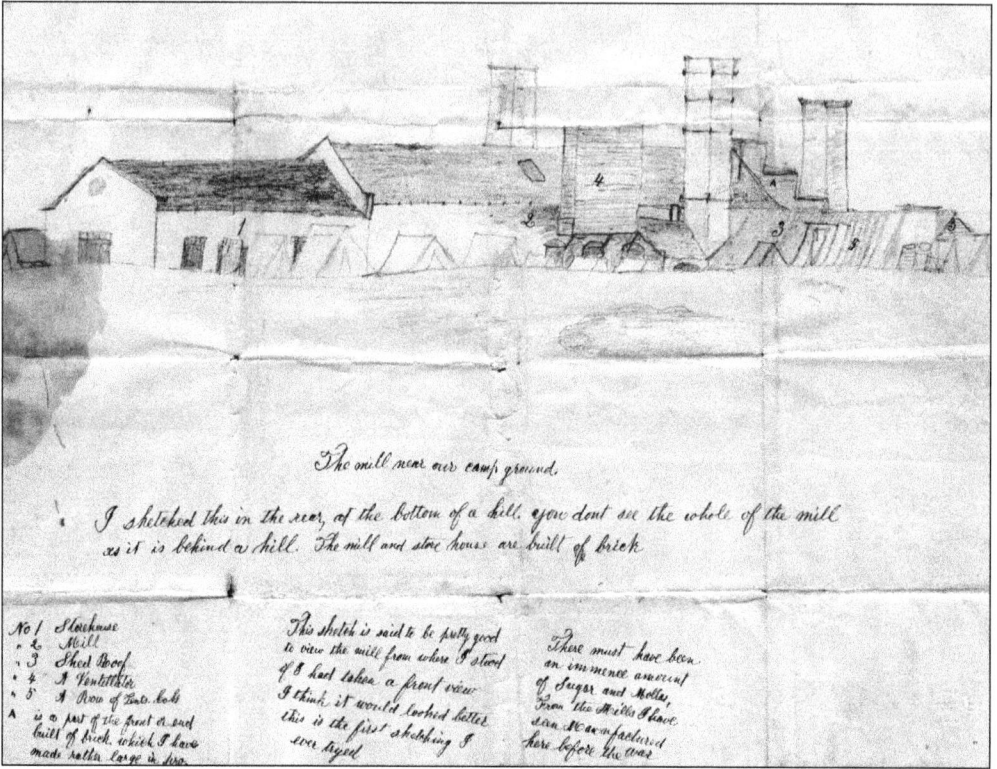

THE MILL NEAR LARRA WENTWORTH'S CAMPGROUND. Larra was an avid writer, even penning a journal of his Civil War experiences. This sketch of a mill near his campground is illustrative of his talent and curiosity. (Courtesy of Peg Wentworth Morse.)

THE BATTLE OF FORT HUDSON. The handwriting on this picture is that of Larra Wentworth of Canton, who fought here. The photograph was taken shortly after the surrender of Port Hudson on July 8, 1863, days after Union victories at Gettysburg and Vicksburg. Port Hudson was located approximately 25 miles north of Baton Rouge. The siege of Port Hudson started on March 14, 1863 and ended July 8. By taking Port Hudson, the Union Army took control of the Mississippi River and divided the Confederacy. (Courtesy of Peg Wentworth Morse.)

KILLED

WALTER S. CLOVER,
AT GAINES MILLS,
JUNE 27, 1862.

JOHN MC GINLEY,
AT BULL RUN,
AUG. 29, 1862.

EDWARD H. R. REVERE,
GEORGE W. KEHR,
AT ANTIETAM,
SEPT. 17, 1862.

JAMES DONAHOE,
ANDREW L. HILL,
AT FREDERICKSBURGH,
DEC. 11–13, 1862.

CHARLES E. BOOTMAN,
STEPHEN H. SMITH,
AT PORT HUDSON,
JUNE 14, 1863.

ROBERT BLACKBURN JR.,
JOHN DENNINGHAM,
JOHN O'BRIEN,
IN THE WILDERNESS,
MAY 5–6, 1864.

CIVIL WAR CASUALTIES. This mural, one of two, is found in the lobby of the town hall. Listed are some of the casualties Canton suffered during the Civil War. Note the two casualties at Port Hudson, whose names were listed by Larra Wentworth in the margin of the picture found on the preceding page.

THE TOMBSTONE OF FREDERIC O. BULLOCK. Frederic Bullock was born in Canton and died in Wisconsin while fighting for the Union Army. He was 20 years old. His remains are buried in Canton Cemetery on Washington Street.

30

LARRA WENTWORTH, CIVIL WAR VETERAN. Larra, like many war veterans, was understandably and justifiably proud of his service to his country. He appears in this photograph dressed in his old uniform. Other than his Civil War travels, he lived in Canton, working as a farmer. He died in 1912. (Courtesy of Peg Wentworth Morse.)

A CIVIL WAR MONUMENT. This statue of a Civil War soldier stands inside of the town hall. Originally outside, it stood in front of the town hall (see pp. 92–93) until the effects of the weather and vandalism drove him to warmer confines.

TONIGHT
Monster VICTORY Parade
MASS MEETING
Band Concert   Fireworks

Brockton Band

MASSAPOAG PARADE GROUNDS

Canton, Massachusetts.

Monday Evening, November 11, 1918

at 7:30 P. M.

ROUTE OF PARADE
Corner Neponset and Washington Streets to Memorial Hall,
Thence to Parade Grounds.

FORMATION OF PARADE
Police, Marshal, Selectmen and Town Officials, Fire Department,
All Soldiers and Sailors in Canton
State Guards, Red Cross, Liberty Loan Committee, Civilian
Men and Women on Washington Street, headed North
at Neponset Street with Flags.

British and French on Neponset Street headed East with Flags.

Italians and Portugese on Church Street headed East with Flags.

Greeks, Lithuanians and Poles on Rockland Street headed West
with Flags.

Hebrews on Mechanic Street headed West with Flags.

Automobiles on Bolivar Street headed West with Flags.

**ALL PERSONS ARE REQUESTED TO BRING AMERICAN
AND ALLIED FLAGS.**

All Bells will please ring and Whistles blow from 7:00 to 7:15.

A WORLD WAR I VICTORY PARADE. To celebrate victory, Canton, like towns throughout the nation, sponsored a large outdoors celebration. Every resident of the town was encouraged to join this huge jubilee. Of interest is the request that citizens of similar nationalities gather together—for instance, Italians on Church Street, Greeks on Rockland. (Courtesy Canton Public Library.)

A WWI Plaque. This plaque, located on Washington Street in front of the Hemenway and across from the post office, commemorates those Canton residents who died in WWI. Note the name of Helen Homans, who died of pneumonia in France. In 1915, she traveled there and joined the French ambulance service. Transferred to various area hospitals, she served near the front line with valor and bravery, ultimately winning high honors from the French government.

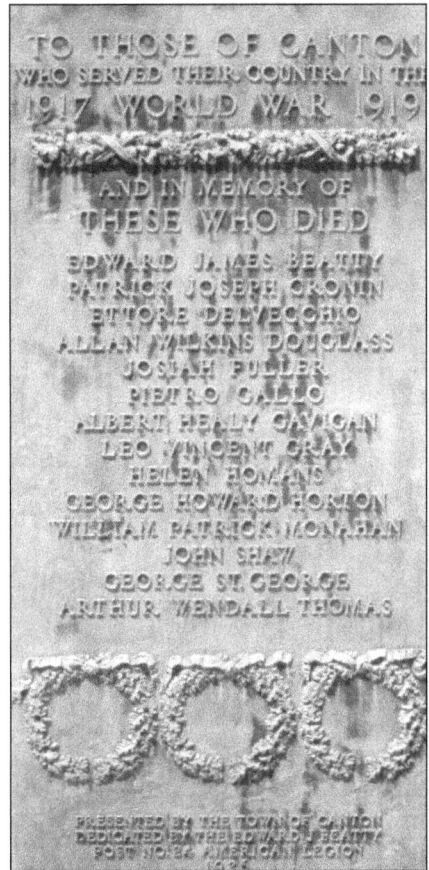

Nathaniel Newcomb Wentworth Jr, 1937. Nathaniel was born in 1917 and died in 1992. He attended Rhode Island State College, where he was a member of ROTC. He fought in WWII (p. 123). (Courtesy of Peg Wentworth Morse.)

HENRY LANE. Sgt. Henry Lane, from Canton, fought in WWII. He contacted tuberculosis and died shortly thereafter. (Courtesy of Jean Galvin.)

STAFF SGT. CHARLES TOLIAS. Some years after graduating from high school (p. 62), Charlie Tolias, at the age of 20, enlisted in the army. On June 6, 1944, his 2nd Ranger Battalion landed in Normandy. Half of his unit did not survive the day. Charlie, however, did survive. Two months before the end of the war, on March 3, 1945, his jeep hit a land mine, resulting in the loss of his legs. At the age of 77, this modest hero was honored by his lifelong home of Canton, when the busy corner of Washington and Bolivar Streets was dedicated as Charles S. Tolias Square. (Courtesy of Charlie Tolias.)

Three

DOWNTOWN CANTON

DOWNTOWN CANTON IN THE EARLY 1930S. This view from the corner of Washington and Neponset Streets looks north to the center of town. The building on the left with the awning, 516 Washington Street, was a small store, which was soon replaced by Chandler's Hardware Store. Chandler's was a fixture in town for many decades, until it closed in 1998. (Courtesy of Edward D. Galvin.)

WASHINGTON STREET, 1905. This serene view looks toward Bolivar Street from the corner of Washington and Rockland Streets. As is readily apparent, downtown Canton at that time was a mixture of businesses and residences. (Courtesy of Dan Keleher.)

WASHINGTON STREET IN THE EARLY 1900S. To accommodate the needs of the local populace, small stores abounded. Frequently, they stayed in business a relatively short time before being converted into a new enterprise. The large elm tree pictured on the right was especially well known; it was cut down due to disease. (Courtesy of Joe DeFelice.)

BROOKS BLOCK. This thriving downtown area was a busy one. The Brooks Building housed, among other things, Moulton's Drug Store, N.E. Telephone, a barbershop, and the Odd Fellows Hall, a social organization whose motto was "Friendship, Love and Truth (FLT)." (Courtesy of Dan Keleher.)

PILCHERS STOVE IN BROOKS BLOCK. This furniture store was located in a convenient spot. Nearby was a small food store as well as a dry goods store. The Masons rented an upstairs room to house their meetings. Note the residential building next-door. (Courtesy of Dan Keleher.)

THE BROOKS BUILDING AREA, EARLY 1900S. This lovely structure was located on the corner of Washington and Bolivar Streets. Like many structures, it too was to suffer the fate of a devastating fire. The complex met its end in 1943. (Courtesy of Joe DeFelice.)

THE BROOKS BUILDING AREA TODAY. Not as grandiose nor noteworthy as its predecessor, this nondescript, one-story building houses some small businesses, including a travel agency. Note the home on the far left in both pictures. Obviously, it has been around for several decades.

THE UNIVERSALIST CHURCH ON WASHINGTON STREET, C. 1900S. To the right of this lovely church stood Sawyer's Hardware. On the far right, the Casey family resided at one point. Officer Casey worked for the police department. (Courtesy of Joe DeFelice.)

THE UNIVERSALIST CHURCH AREA TODAY. The view today is neither as lovely nor inviting as it once was. In the place of a graceful church, a market now sits. Instead of the elegant Brooks Building, a single-story business complex exists.

A Parade on Washington Street, early 1900s. The parade is heading out of Canton in the direction of the library. The building on the left front is the Canton Catholic Club, at one point known as the Massapoag House. (Courtesy of Jean Galvin.)

Canton Catholic Club, Canton, Mass.

A Catholic Club. The Canton Catholic Club, established in 1908, catered to the social needs of all peoples. The facility had reading rooms, pool and billiard rooms, a bowling alley, lecture hall, sleeping facilities, as well as dancing and moving pictures. The highly popular spot burned down on January 5, 1918, a day so cold that all of the fire hydrants were frozen. Today, the post office occupies this site. (Courtesy of Ann Galvin.)

THE WENTWORTH MARKET. Billy Wentworth owned the buckboard on the left. Edward Wentworth is sitting in the St. Louis delivery truck to the right. Sawyer's Hardware Store stood to the left of Wentworth Market. The buildings were located on the corner of Mechanic and Washington Streets. In this area today are a liquor store and the Bank of Canton. (Courtesy of Peg Wentworth Morse.)

AN OLD HOME WEEK PARADE. This c. 1910 parade features the town's fire department. The picture is taken from the vantage point of Washington and Bolivar Streets. Today, the Rose Deli occupies this location. The Richard Lewis clothing store is on the left. (Courtesy of Jean Galvin.)

POLICE MARCHING, C. 1913. The police department was founded in 1875. Four police officers were hired on a budget of $434. The main crimes centered around alcohol violations. Included here is John H. Flood, who was hired in 1896 and became chief in 1913, serving until his death in 1935. The other officers are John Braverman, who was hired in 1911; Thomas Kannally; and William Casey, who was hired c. 1913. (Courtesy of Jean Galvin.)

A HORSE-DRAWN APPARATUS, C. 1910–1912. This parade is traveling by the corner of Washington and Bolivar Streets. Until the mid-1880s, the fire department was made up mainly of volunteers. Often fires were not fought, due simply to an inability to do so; fires frequently burned themselves out. (Courtesy of Canton Public Library.)

FIREMEN, C. 1910–1912. Technological advances professionalized the fire department. With the emergence of the water department came the ability to create and organize fire hydrants. The town saw the need to move from volunteers toward full-time professionals, which greatly improved the ability to fight fires. (Courtesy of Canton Public Library.)

A JULY FOURTH PARADE. The 1930 celebration of our nation's birthday featured a parade on Washington Street. The 25 floats included those devoted to the Apostle John Eliot; Roger Sherman, an author and signer of the Declaration of Independence; Deborah Sampson, who posed as a male so she could fight in the Revolutionary War; Paul Revere; and the Doty Tavern where independence and war were debated by delegates from several towns and districts. (Courtesy of Canton Public Library.)

WASHINGTON AND BOLIVAR STREETS, C. 1930s. This was one of Canton's first major blocks. At one point, Dr. Luce (for whom the Dean S. Luce Elementary School would eventually be named) had his medical office in one of the upstairs suites. In one of the first floor storefronts, a fruit store existed, run by a somewhat interesting character whom local residents called "Auntie Peanuts." (Courtesy of Rick Saquet.)

A MODERN VIEW. This area has changed remarkably little over the years. Today, a hair salon, a coffee shop, and clothing stores occupy the space.

WASHINGTON STREET UNDER REPAIR, 1947. In 1947, the main street of Canton underwent significant renovations. On the right, Mario's, an eating establishment, existed. Today, another Italian restaurant, Rosario's, stands in its place. (Courtesy of Joe DeFelice.)

JENNEY, 1947. Jenney was a gas station. Across the street, White's Market stood in the area of today's 7-11 store. White's Market, like many markets at the time, sold meats and vegetables. (Courtesy of Joe DeFelice.)

MOBIL GAS, 1947. Morse and Mullen Automobile (p. 109) was also located in this area. Dunkin' Donuts is there today. In the upstairs of the building straight ahead, existed the Italian Club, which was a social and fraternal organization for those of Italian descent. (Courtesy of Joe DeFelice.)

WHITE'S MARKET, 1947. The apartments above White's housed some of the earliest members of Canton's minority community. The *Canton Journal*, a local paper in existence for over a century, was located to the left of White's. Still farther down were the offices of Dr. Billings, a local dentist. (Courtesy of Joe DeFelice.)

WASHINGTON AND WALL STREETS, 1947. Owned by the Titus family, the Washington Street Liquor Store was called Big D's. This view looks toward Cobbs corner. (Courtesy of Joe DeFelice.)

A MODERN VIEW. The liquor store has moved to across the street, next to the Bank of Canton, while Strand Jewelers occupies what was once the liquor store. Next to Strand's is a building that has been boarded-up.

THE CANTON MARKET, C. 1970S. At one time, this market was called Pozzo's Market. It was located across from the library until it was replaced by Kramer Jewelers and the Brockton Credit Union. (Courtesy of Ann Galvin.)

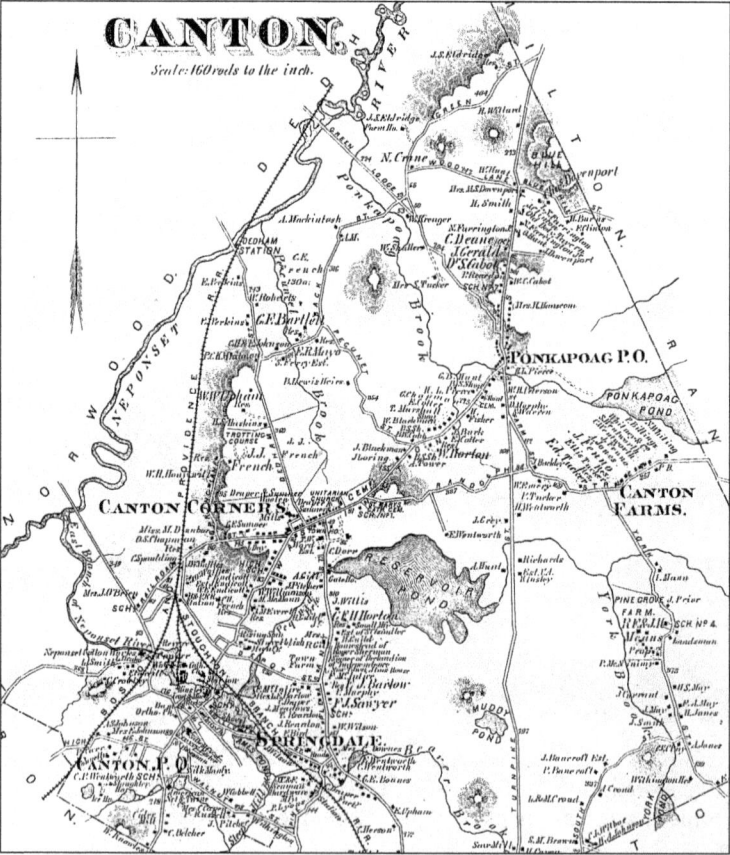

MAP OF CANTON, c. 1876. This map shows Canton as it appeared 1876. (Courtesy of Kay Gleason of Historical Inc., www. oldmapsne.com.)

Four

SCHOOLS

ELIOT SCHOOL, 1940. This photograph shows the eighth-grade class at the Eliot School, which was built in 1894. The prior Eliot School on this site was built in 1867. Located at 1492 Washington Street, today it serves as town office space. The school was named for the Apostle John Eliot, who first preached the gospel to Native Americans on September 14, 1646 in the wigwam of Kitchamakin. (Courtesy of Canton Public Library.)

CANTON'S FIRST HIGH SCHOOL. Canton's first high school cost $10,000 to build and was opened in 1869. It would last approximately 40 years before the population of the town required a new building. The building was made of wood and consisted of two floors. Today, a Getty gas station on Washington Street stands in its place. (Courtesy of Joe DeFelice.)

THE CANTON HIGH SCHOOL CLASS OF 1911. This photograph was taken on May 24, 1909, in front of what was then the high school. The students who signed the back of the photograph include Elsie W. Poole, Rachael A. Hewett, Laura B. Curtis, Amelia Guild, Winifred Drislain, Mary A. Fenno, Helen T. Gerald, Doris McRitchie, Prescott W. Lentell, Alfred E. Hughes, Gladys M. Smith, Edward McMorrow, Frank K. Haszard, Ethel J. Blanc, Mildred E. Stone, and Marion Weir. For a view of how some of these students appeared in elementary school, see page 64. (Courtesy of Al D'Attanasio.)

REPORT OF THE COMMITTEE

Appointed at the Annual Town Meeting, March 7, 1910,

to investigate and report on sites available for a

NEW HIGH SCHOOL BUILDING.

To the Inhabitants of the Town of Canton:

THE Committee, appointed to investigate and report on sites available for a new high school building, has made a careful inspection of the different pieces of property that have been suggested. Some of these properties were found to be undesirable for the purpose and others that seemed to be suitable were not available as the owners refused to sell for school purposes or for other reasons. The committee presents the following list of properties, all of which are located on Washington Street, with a brief statement of the qualifications of each:

(1.) PROPERTY OF MRS. HELEN M. TOLMAN: (on westerly side of Washington Street between Neponset and Church Streets)

The committee made a personal examination of this lot and found it unsuitable. In order to provide sufficient room for a high school building and grounds it would be necessary to purchase several adjoining properties and remove at least eight buildings. It was decided that the expense of procuring this site would be prohibitive and no attempt was made to obtain prices from the various owners.

(2.) PROPERTY OF THE HEIRS OF FRANK M. AMES: (Washington and Revere Streets.) This land, containing about four acres, has a frontage of 291 feet on Washington Street and 480 feet on Revere Street. This lot is of adequate size with sufficient room not only for a school building, but for playgrounds for out-of-door sports. It is centrally located as regards school population and convenient to the Public Library. The front half of the lot where the School house would stand is in excellent condition and the grading facilities are extremely good. The rear of the lot consists of a series of ledges, partly covered, rising a few feet above the general level of the lot. This section could be improved and beautified so as to add to, rather than detract from the general appearance of the site. A serious objection to the selection of this site is its proximity to the property formerly of the Kinsley Iron and Machine Company and other manufacturing properties, the future de-

THE 1910 NEW HIGH SCHOOL REPORT. As this nearly century-old study reveals, locating and planning for additional schools is an ongoing, never-ending consideration for any town, including Canton. As the Crane High School was being overextended, calls for a new high school echoed. Ultimately, after some controversy over the location, option No. 2 was selected. A major factor was a contribution of $20,000 by Augustus Hemenway. (Courtesy of Canton Public Library.)

HEMENWAY HIGH SCHOOL. The Hemenway School was named for Augustus Hemenway, one who gave much to the town. The Class of 1912 was the first class to graduate from this stately setting. After the school closed, it was eventually converted into elderly housing. (Courtesy of Joe DeFelice.)

THE PRESENT-DAY HIGH SCHOOL. In its earliest days, the land upon which the current Canton High School stands was the site of Native American tribal meetings held by Sachem Chief Ahauton. In the 1800s, it was the site of the Morse and French estates. Today, in the front of the school, a WWII memorial marks Canton's contribution to the war effort. (Courtesy of Joe DeFelice.)

FINANCIAL REPORT.

TEACHERS' SALARIES.

HIGH SCHOOL.

Frederic L. Owen, Jr...................$1,200 00		
Eliza R. Noyes........................ 535 00		
	————	$1,735 00

ELIOT SCHOOL.

Nelson Freeman........................$380 00		
Abram T. Smith........................ 570 00		
Ellen Clarke......................... 384 00		
Ida J. Capen......................... 360 00		
Eliza A. Sumner...................... 400 00		
Ellen M. Cronon...................... 25 00		
	————	$2,119 00

PONKAPOAG SCHOOL.

Mary O. Wentworth.....................$344 00		
Maggie J. Kailher.................... 95 00		
	————	$439 00

CRANE SCHOOL.

Charles H. Morse......................$950 00		
Ellen E. Kelley...................... 360 00		
Lucie A. Hall........................ 400 00		
Julia A. Crane....................... 240 00		

THE 1885 TEACHER SALARIES. This is the first page of a two-page report on teacher salaries in 1885. Needless to say, they did not make a lot of money. There were eight schools in Canton: the high school (2 teachers), the Eliot School (6 teachers), the Ponkapoag School (2 teachers), the Crane School (14 teachers), the York School (1 teacher), the Sherman School (1 teacher), the Revere School (3 teachers), and the Gridley School (2 teachers). (Courtesy of Peg Wentworth Morse.)

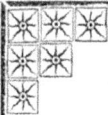

CANTON

GRAMMAR SCHOOLS

CONCERT
- - - - - AND - - - - -
GRADUATION.

Memorial Hall,

Wednesday Eve'g, June 24, '96.

THE 1896 GRAMMER SCHOOL GRADUATION PROGRAM. At the town hall on June 24, 1896, at 7:45 in the evening, the Eliot School, the Crane School, and the York School held their grammer school graduation. Thirteen students graduated from the Eliot School, while 17 graduated from the Crane. The York School saw but a single graduate—Alfretta Crowd. (Courtesy of Canton Public Library.)

St. John's Graduation, c. 1910. Rev. John J. Farrell served as St. John's third pastor from 1909 until 1918. Father Farrell contributed greatly to the success of the Canton Catholic Club (p. 40). Father Farrell also established the Holy Name Society and the archdiocese's first Fife and Drum Corps. In 1918, he was transferred to St. Paul's Church in Dorchester. (Courtesy of Jean Galvin.)

St. John's Graduation, 1921. Rev. Mark E. Madden, who had been the parish priest at St. Philip's Church in Boston, replaced Father Farrell in 1919 and served St. John's until 1934, when he was transferred to St. John's in Winthrop. Under his leadership, the convent of the Sisters of St. Joseph was erected (it was torn down in 1996), and both the St. John's school and church itself were remodeled and renovated. Like Father Farrell, Father Madden also served as a trustee to the public library. (Courtesy of Jean Galvin.)

REVERE STREET GRAMMER SCHOOL, EARLY 1900S. Over the years, Canton has had a variety of elementary schools. The Revere Street School building is still in existence near the Canton Junction train station. It currently houses a garden and landscaping business. (Courtesy of Peg Morse Wentworth.)

THE CANTON HIGH SCHOOL CLASS OF 1924. Needless to say, the graduating class size of Canton High School has increased since 1924. The Class of 2000 graduated 154 students, which does not include the many high school seniors who live in the town, but attend private schools elsewhere. In this 1924 photograph, Charles Moss appears in the top row, the second from left. His grandson, Jeff Curran, lives in Canton, continuing the family tradition. (Courtesy of Jeff Curran.)

56

St. John's High School Class of 1926. Of the 14 graduates, one was a male. The following year, the church underwent substantial renovations, the plans being made by Boston architect and church parishioner Matthew Sullivan. Among other changes, a carved wooden alter and rail were installed, and the original windows were replaced by stained-glass ones. (Courtesy of Ann Galvin.)

Mike Cohen, c. 1930s. As a childhood joke, Edward Manning Cohen's friends called him Mike. The name stuck, and to his death he was known to one and all as Mike. Few actually knew his true name. Pictured here in the 1930s, Mike played football for Canton High School. He remained in Canton, working for many decades at Connors furniture store on Route 138. (Courtesy of Cohen Family.)

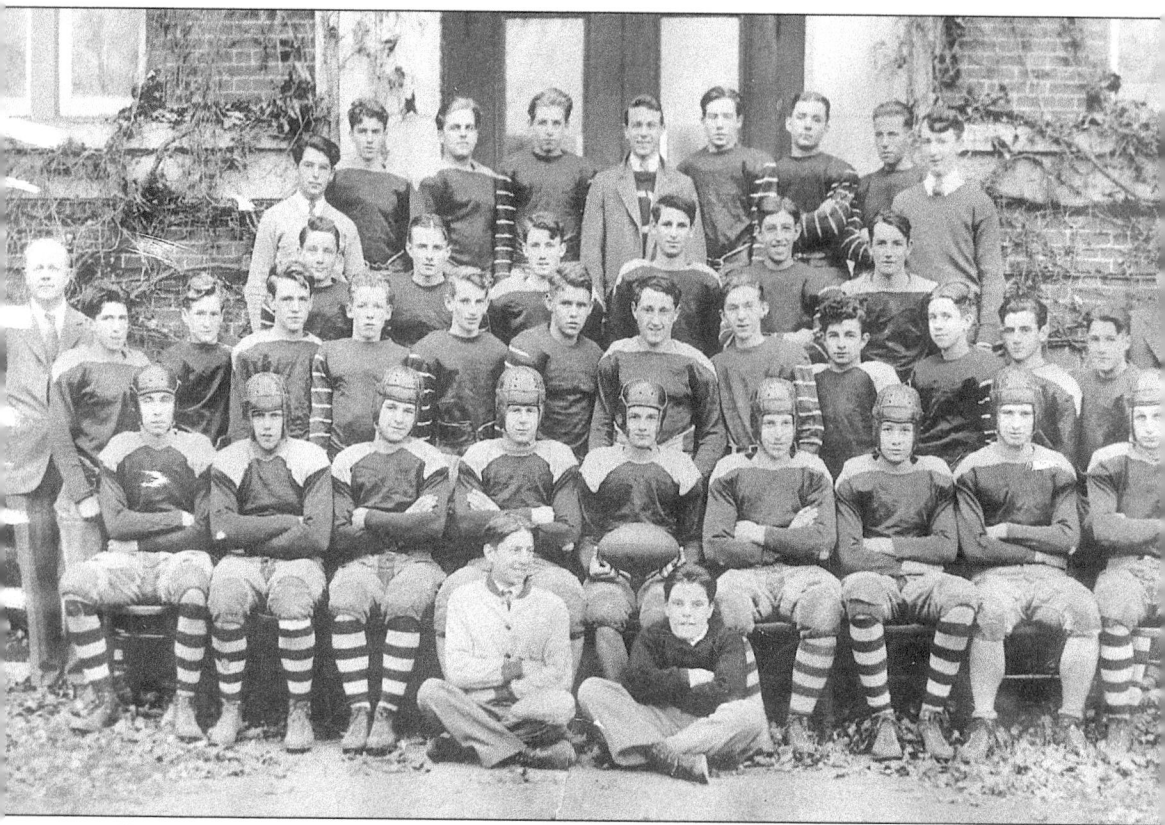

THE CANTON HIGH SCHOOL FOOTBALL TEAM, C. 1931. Charlie Stevenson was one of Canton High School's greatest quarterbacks. Pictured in the first row of players, the fifth from the left, Stevenson started the third game of his sophomore season and over the next three years, would only lose two games. In 1929, he led Canton to its first victory ever over rival Stoughton 19–0. Charlie still lives in Canton. Grandfather to nine, he has ten great-grandchildren. On a more sobering note, Walter Berteletti (second row of players, second from the right) was killed in WWII. (Courtesy of Charlie Stevenson.)

THE CANTON HIGH SCHOOL BASEBALL TEAM, C. 1932. Charlie Stevenson (second row, fifth player from left) also played baseball. One of his teammates was one of Canton's truly great ball players, baseball captain Bob Gibson. Pictured in the third row, the fourth player from the left, Gibson was honored when the high school baseball field was named for him. Gibson went to Boston University, where he played baseball, football, and ran track. He is also a member of the Baseball Coaches Association Hall of Fame. He served in the U.S. Navy from 1942 to 1946. Principal "Baldy" Hall (second row, far left) and legendary coach Bill Donovan (second row, far right) are also pictured. (Courtesy of Charlie Stevenson.)

THE 50TH ANNIVERSARY OF ST. JOHN'S FIRST GRADUATING CLASS. The first class to graduate from St. John's was the Class of 1888. Fifty years later, on January 27, 1938, the class gathered

REUNION
OF THE FORMER PUPILS
ST. JOHN'S SCHOOL, CANTON
AND CELEBRATION OF THE
FIFTIETH ANNIVERSARY
OF THE SCHOOL'S FIRST GRADUATION
OF 1888
MEMORIAL HALL, CANTON, MASS., JAN. 27/

to celebrate that event. The party was held on the second floor of the town hall, which easily accommodated the masses assembled. (Courtesy of Briget Meehan.)

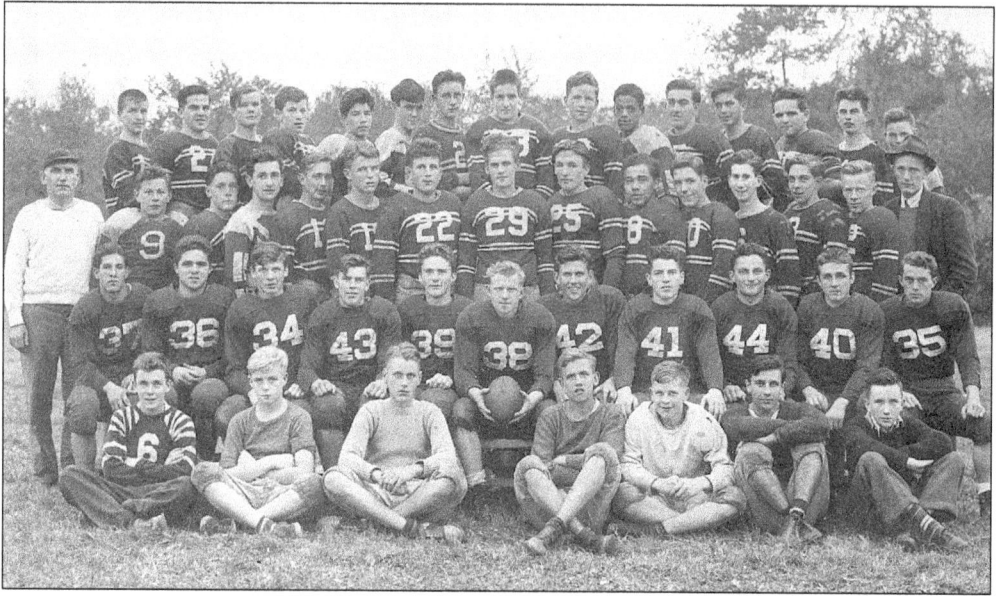

THE 1940 CANTON HIGH SCHOOL FOOTBALL TEAM. In one of the greatest upsets in the history of the Canton-Stoughton football rivalry, which started in 1926, Canton defeated the undefeated and unscored-on Stoughton 6–0 in the last game of the 1940 season. As reported by the *Canton Journal*, on fourth down, halfback Antoine Gomes scored, on Canton's fourth attempt, from a yard out on a hole opened up by left guard Charlie Tolias (second row, far left) Tolias also appears on page 34. (Courtesy of Charlie Tolias.)

ST. JOHN'S CLASS OF 1942. The six students who graduated from St. John's on June 14, 1942, comprised the smallest graduating class in the state, if not the nation. Shown, from left to right, are Mary Kelleher, Christina Phillips, Paul Danahy, Msgr. Robert E. Lee, Francis Raftery, Rita Gorman, and Alice Buckley. (Courtesy of Blanche Nervi.)

THE GRIDLEY SCHOOL. Named after Maj. Gen. Richard Gridley (1710–1796), who lived throughout his life in the immediate area, the Gridley School opened in 1854 and closed in 1964. The two-story building had grades one through three on the first floor, while grades four through six were on the second story. Generally, two teachers tended to the needs of all of the students. The school was recently renovated and currently houses a preschool. General Gridley served in the Revolutionary War and was the founder of the Army Corps of Engineers.

FIRST GRADERS AT THE GRIDLEY SCHOOL. In 1956, Peg Wentworth (front row, far right) attended Mrs. Betteti's first-grade class at the Gridley School. Peg lived in the same house as her great-grandparents nearly two centuries before. She also attended the Hemenway School, the Canton High School, and Hood College. Married, with two children, three horses, two dogs, a cat, and a rabbit, she now lives in Wrentham managing a retail farm stand and apple orchard with her husband. (Courtesy of Peg Wentworth Morse.)

THE CRANE SCHOOL. The Crane School, named for Elijah Crane, was located where Walgreens is today. It was a red brick building set back in the lot. As one might imagine, it had grass in its front yard. Its steps, leading to Washington Street, are still in existence. (Courtesy of Canton Public Library.)

NINTH-GRADE GRADUATES OF THE CRANE SCHOOL, 1907. Some of the students who graduated here went on to graduate from Canton High School four years later (p. 50). They include Elsie Poole, Marion Weir, Laura Curtis, Gladys Smith, Mary Fenno, Mildred Stone, and Ethel Blanc. The principal was E.E. Kelley. (Courtesy of Al D'Attanasio.)

A PARTY AT THE CRANE SCHOOL. Canton Center was the place to be on a Saturday evening. Regardless of what section of Canton one lived in, if action was sought, traveling to the center was a necessity. The Crane School was torn down in 1955. (Courtesy of Canton Public Library.)

WILLIAM H. GALVIN, BOSTON COLLEGE CLASS OF 1932. The Galvin Middle School in Canton is named for the young man pictured here. Dr. Galvin started his long educational career as a teacher at the high school in 1935. He was a principal at three Canton schools, including the Crane (1943–1950), the Hemenway (1950–1954), and the Luce (1954–1958). He served one year as assistant superintendent of schools before being named superintendent in 1959. The Galvin Middle School was dedicated on September 30, 1973. (Courtesy of Ann Galvin.)

THE MASSACHUSETTS HOSPITAL SCHOOL. This specialized school opened in 1915 to cater to children with special needs. It continues to this day with that mission. The design of the facility was somewhat controversial and avant garde when it opened. (Courtesy of Joe DeFelice.)

DR. JOHN C. FISH ADDRESSES CROWD. The founder, builder, and superintendent of the Massachusetts Hospital School addresses an audience at the celebration of Canton's 150th anniversary in 1947. He was at the school for more than 40 years. He died a year after this photograph was taken. Services, conducted by Rev. Richard Warren and Rev. Thomas A. Sinclair, were held at the Unitarian Church. (Courtesy of Canton Public Library.)

LIBRARY READING, 1947. On May 9, 1947, Judith Draper of the Horigon Club reads *Mrs. Piggle Wiggle* to schoolchildren in grades one through five at the town hall. From the children's expressions, some appear to be gaining more from the experience than others. (Courtesy of Canton Public Library.)

ST JOHN'S 1944 EIGHTH GRADE GRADUATING CLASS. Shown, from left to right, are the following: (front row) Shirley Libby, Claire McEnaney, Antoinette Daganiero, Phyllis Banks, Msgr. Lee, Mary Brown, Jean Parker, Bertha LeBarre, and Blanche Danahy; (middle row) Guy Digirolamo, Paul Graham, Ralph DeMayo, George Smith, James Galvin, Paul Healy, Leo Johnson, Robert Farrell, Joseph Gilmore, Robert Martineau, James Downey, John Flanagan, and Raymond Sweeney; (back row) Sam Fama, Ann Marie O'Brien, Maureen Dallahan, Marilyn Galligan, Ann P. Collins, Jean Becherer, Frances McDermott, Ann C. Collins, and Vincent Digirolamo. (Courtesy of Jean Galvin.)

THE CANTON HIGH SCHOOL CLASS OF 1948 CLASS TRIP TO WASHINGTON, D.C. Shown, from left to right, are the following: (front row) Paul Healy, Vincent Digirolamo, Jim Dowling, Paul Graham, Lee Thackwray, Henry Johnson, Harold Tate, Gerald Sherr, Jack Flanagan, "Topsy" Burke, Sam Fama, John Lomartere, Ralph DeMayo, "Cliff" Lewis, George Olden, Fred Nelson, and Jim Callanan; (middle row) Doris Eveline, Ann C. Collins, Maureen Dallahan, Alyce Geissler, Jean Becherer, Esther Morandi, Doris Doody, Jean Parker, Marilyn Galligan, Mary

Burtkus, Blanche Danahy, Charlotte Doody, Wilma Caron, Natalie Dray, Ann Marie O'Brien, Ann P. Collins, Margaret Conlon, and Charlotte Lowry; (back row) the busdriver, Harold Croft, Sam Mitchell, Leo Johnson, Nancy Merriam, Jane Buckley, Louise Copley, unidentified, Miss Roache, Mrs. Dana, Mr. Scully, Miss Johnson, Don Russell, Jack Eaton, Jack Porter, "Gus" Broderick, Robert Farrell, George Smith, and Frances McDermott. (Courtesy of Jean Galvin)

THE CANTON HIGH SCHOOL CLASS OF 1948. Many of the students who graduated from St. John's eighth-grade class in 1944 continued their education at Canton High School, which saw its class join them from the Crane and Eliot Schools. (Courtesy of Jean Galvin.)

THE 50TH REUNION OF CANTON HIGH SCHOOL CLASS OF 1948. Shown, from left to right, are the following: (first row) Jane (Buckley) Bent, Louise (Copley) Gronsoor, Charlotte (Doody) Zucca, Jean (Parker) MacDonald, Leo Johnson, Blanche (Danahy) Nervi, Doris (Doody) Lawrie, and Charlotte (Lowry) Perez; (second row) George Olden, Ann (Collins) Piana, Jean (Becherer) Galvin, Doris (Eveline) DeCambra, Esther (Galligan) Kelley, Anne (O'Brien) Magee, Ethel (Lehto) Powell, Priscilla (O'Dell) Page, Mary (Burtkus) Shannon, and Paul Healy; (third row) Tony Menino, Jack Eaton, Don Russell, John Fralic, Louise (Withers) McCort, Wilma (Caron) Bernarde, Nancy (Merriam) Grafton, and Bill Cole; (top row) Russell Leeman, George Smith, Vincent Digirolamo, Sam Fama, Dick Witt, John Lomartere, and Bernard LeBarre. (Courtesy of Jean Galvin.)

PROM NIGHT, 1948. Jean Becherer went to the prom with class president Leo Johnson, who was voted the best dressed and neatest student of his class. He also played football and basketball. Jean, noted for her brains and beauty, was chosen as Canton's representative to Girls' State. She ultimately married Jack Galvin. Among her children are Massachusetts Rep. Bill Galvin, Canton Police Sgt. Liz Galvin, and local insurance man Joe Galvin. (Courtesy of Jean Galvin.)

MRS. WARREN'S COMMUNITY KINDERGARTEN, 1950–1951. Shown, from left to right, are the following: (front row) Richard Curtis, Carol Ann Basanquet, Donna Lee Brown, Carol Bright, Judy O'Neil, and Michael Warren; (back row) Billy Dickie, Jimmy Bougas, Wicky Carpenter, Paul Hagan, Nat Wentworth, and Peter Bright. Peter is currently the Canton police chief. (Courtesy of Peg Wentworth Morse.)

CANTON HIGH SCHOOL CHEERLEADERS, 1952. Shown, from left to right, are the following: (front row) Mary Matthews, J. Burke, and Audrey Moss; (back row) Mary Callahan, Helen Dean, Shirley Flannagan, J. Doody, Alice (Dorothy?) Cleveland, and Helen Marilyn Howard. (Courtesy of Mona Podgurski.)

The New

DEAN S. LUCE SCHOOL

THE DEAN S. LUCE ELEMENTARY SCHOOL. Dr. Luce was one of two doctors in Canton during WWII. Given that reality, his job was a busy and never-ending one. In appreciation to his many long and selfless hours, this elementary school, opened in the mid-1950s, was named after him. A major, new addition was completed on the facility in the year 2000. (Courtesy of Canton Public Library.)

THE FIRST LUCE FACULTY, 1954–1955. Shown, from left to right, are the following: (front row) Mae Roach, Dee DiBenedetto, Kay Finn, Jeanne Rosengard, Claire Lyons, Alice ?, and Marie Whitty; (middle row) Barbara McKay, unidentified, custodian Frank Cobb, George Farnham, principal William Galvin, Ed Bowles, Irene Arlinger, and Sylvia Alexander; (back row) Mildred Baril, Rosemary Sebert, Florence Horn, Ann O'Neil, Marilyn Glynn, Mary Nask, and Lavina Dallahan. (Courtesy of Ann Galvin.)

THE FIRST LUCE EIGHTH GRADERS, 1954–1955. Shown, from left to right, are the following: (first row) Richard Dray, Frederick White, Jerry Kelleher, David Fleming, and Charles Wendell; (second row) Susan Curra, Noel Upham, Edna Jean Comer, Annmarie Tardaico, Joan Vitelli, Patricia Hicks, Judith Dumaine, Susan Cleveland, and Beverley Noll; (third row) teacher Ed Bowles, John Colson, David Thomas, Arthur Radden, Elizabeth Taylor, Judith Layman, Sandra Standish, Christine Lundgren, Robert O'Brien, David Macbeth, Roger Hall, and principal William Galvin; (fourth row) Steven Burnham, Paul Shea, Kenneth MacKenzie, David O'Keefe, Donald Baril, Edwin Banks, Allen Freedman, Peter Carlson, and Dennis Brooks. (Courtesy of Ann Galvin.)

THE 1957 LUCE BASKETBALL TEAM. This rather large basketball squad, numbering 16 children, is evidence of the school's commitment to its youth. Today, the Luce School, along with the other two elementary schools in town—the Kennedy and the Hanson—have multiple teams, consisting of both boys and girls. All three elementary schools teach children from kindergarten through the fifth grade. Afterward, they all go to the Galvin Middle School, grades six through eight. (Courtesy of Ann Galvin.)

THE 1966 LUCE FIRST GRADERS. The mark of a well-respected town is that those who live there stay. Case in point is the Hill-Smith family. John Hill (top row, far left) and his sister, Chrissy, grew up in Canton. Chrissy Smith went to the Luce, Galvin Middle School, and Canton High School, Class of 1982. Her two children are following her footsteps; one is currently in the Galvin, the other in the Luce. (Courtesy of Chrissy Smith.)

THE GALVIN SCHOOL BUILDING COMMITTEE, 1973. Shown, from left to right, are the following: (sitting) M. Ruth Ruane (school committee), Chairman Clifford Seresky, and Margaret Brayton, EdD (school committee); (standing) Joe DeFelice Jr. (planning board chair, p. 127); Gerald Bradley (planning board); Richard Simons; superintendent William Galvin; Theodore J. Goodman, M.D. (school committee chair); Duncan Gillis Jr.; and Sheila Cleimets (selectman chair). (Courtesy of Joe DeFelice)

A STATE HOUSE VISIT. This photograph, taken on the steps inside the State House in Boston, shows the Hansen School elementary class of teacher Ann Galvin (front right). In the center is their host, Massachusetts Rep. Jack Flood, a resident of Canton. Representative Flood unsuccessfully ran for governor prior to his being named sheriff of Norfolk County, a post he later relinquished. Ann Galvin, after 31 years in classroom 204—her room since the school opened in 1969—retired in 2000. Her retirement ended a legacy; there had been a Galvin in the Canton schools since 1936. (Courtesy of Ann Galvin.)

Five

CHURCHES

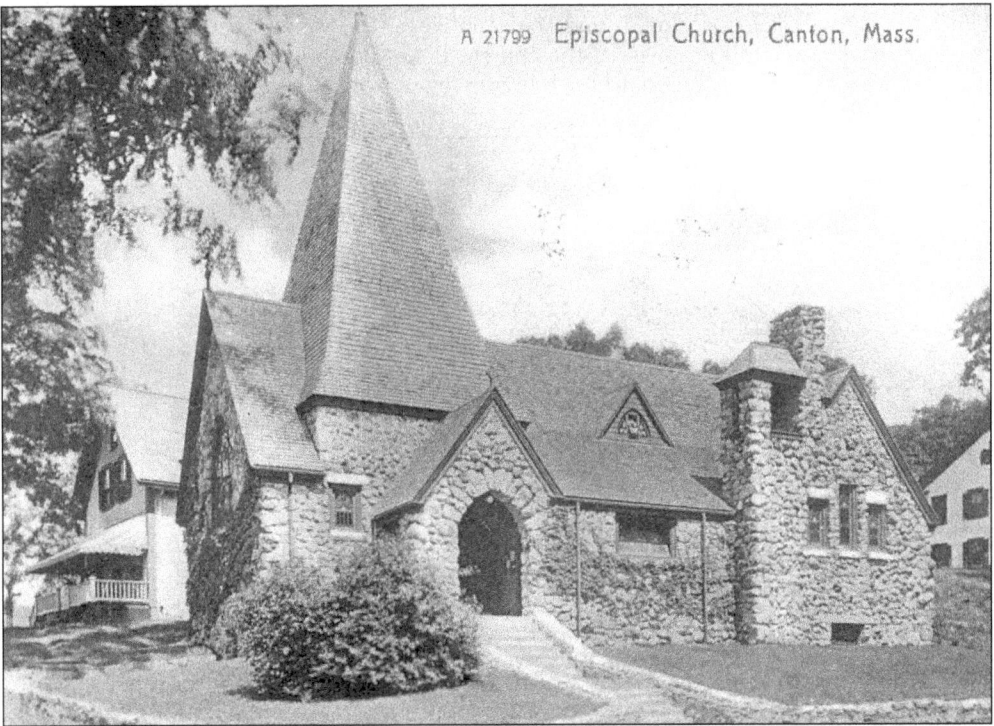

THE EPISCOPAL (TRINITY) CHURCH. This easily recognizable building is now the Schlossberg-Solomon Funeral Home located on the corner of Washington and Chapel Streets, not far from the high school. Erected in 1897, it cost about $5,000 to build. Its bell had been taken by union soldiers in New Orleans and sent to Canton, along with other bells, to be recast as cannons. However, it was spared due to its lyrical nature and found a home in the Revere Copper Yard for 40 years before being donated to the church. A new Trinity church was built in 1969 on land at the corner of Route 138 and Blue Hill River Road. (Courtesy of Ann Galvin.)

THE MEETINGHOUSE OF THE FIRST PRECINCT OF CANTON AND THE SURROUNDING AREA, 1823.
Until the early 1820s, the church and state, unlike today, were closely linked. Typically,
the townspeople were all members of the church. It was not surprising, therefore, that town
meetings were held in the church, whose bills were often paid with public money. (Courtesy of
Canton Public Library.)

THE CONGREGATIONAL MEETINGHOUSE. This house of worship, also pictured above, was
opened in the mid-1740s. Its charismatic and strong leader Pastor Samuel Dunbar, fluent in
Latin, Greek, and Hebrew, graduated Harvard in 1723, arrived in Canton four years later, and
presided over his flock for more than half a century. (Courtesy of Canton Public Library.)

THE ENGLISH CHURCH AND BURYING GROUND. Daniel Huntoon, in his epic *History of Canton*, published in 1893, devoted an entire chapter to the English Church. Suffice it to say that the church fell in disrepair and ultimate destruction after the Revolutionary War. Interestingly, in the graveyard forever lies fervent patriots entombed next to unyielding Tories.

1814   CENTENNIAL   1914

OF THE

FIRST BAPTIST CHURCH

CANTON, MASSACHUSETTS

JUNE TWENTY-FIRST AND TWENTY-SECOND

1914.

THE FIRST BAPTIST CHURCH. In 1914, this church celebrated its 100th anniversary. Unfortunately, the church fell on hard times and closed in 1932. Eerily and symbolic of its situation, its steeple came tumbling down during a storm in the 1930s. The building, located on Church Street in downtown Canton, is still in existence today, having been sold to the Blue Hill Lodge of Masons. (Courtesy of Canton Public Library.)

THE UNIVERSALIST CHURCH. Today, the Canton Market on Washington Street occupies the land where this lovely structure was once a landmark. It opened its doors in the late 1840s. Given the similarity of views with the Unitarian Church, the two merged in 1974. The church was torn down three years later. Its bell was removed to its new location at 1508 Washington Street (p. 81). (Courtesy of Peter Sarra.)

A SUNDAY SCHOOL CLASS, 1915–1916. Members of the "Blue Bird Club" include, from left to right, the following: (first row) Ruby Marden, Wilhememia Fischer, and Ruth Eggleston; (middle row) Irma Wayland, Melba Eggleston, and Dorothy McKee (p. 123); (back row) Georgia Dears, Emma Allen, and Dorthy Dunbar. (Courtesy of Peg Wentworth Morse.)

THE FIRST UNITARIAN CHURCH. Still standing today on Washington Street, this facility opened in 1824. However, the church has been in existence in Canton a great deal longer—since 1717. It merged with the Universalist Church in 1961. The Eliot School is in the background. (Courtesy of Peter Sarra)

THE UNITARIAN-UNIVERSALIST CHURCH TODAY. This area has changed remarkably little over the last century, other than a huge increase of traffic on Washington Street.

THE CONGREGATIONAL CHURCH. The Congregational church was built for under $7,000 in 1860 on Neponset Street, near Washington Street. After 100 years, the lovely building started to feel the effects of time and progress. Too small to address all of the needs of its congregation and with a shortage of parking, it relocated to its present location, shown below, in the early 1960s. In 1969, it was sold to the Mobil Oil Corporation for $50,000. (Courtesy of Peter Sarra.)

THE UNITED CHURCH OF CHRIST. In 1961, the church planning committee recommended spending $45,000 to acquire 8 acres of property to build and relocate its congregation to what is now 1541 Washington Street. It was then that the church also changed its name. Pastor Zdenek F. Bednar, a survivor of a Nazi slave labor camp, guided its development.

THE PONKAPOAG UNION CHAPEL. Opened in 1878, it still stands on Washington Street. While it initially catered mainly to the residents of Ponkapoag, its doors were open to all, both for religious and non-religious purposes. To that end, the Ponkapoag Civil Association held its first meetings there in the mid-1940s. From 1962 to 1966, the newly created James Lutheran Church leased the premises to conduct their services.

BETH ABRAHAM. Jewish families first started arriving in Canton in the mid-1880s. A Temple first opened at 58 Revere Street in 1917. Thanks to the vision and generosity of Abraham Brightman, a successful wool manufacturer, the temple pictured here moved to 731 Washington Street in 1920, where it remained until 1965. In that year, the temple moved to its current quarters at 1301 Washington Street. Today, a Texaco gas station stands at 731 Washington Street. (Courtesy of Peter Sarra.)

ST. JOHN'S CHURCH AND RECTORY. After several attempts at establishing a parish, one was permanently founded in 1861. Shortly thereafter, to accommodate a quickly expanding flock, Father Flatley helped arrange the purchase of the present church property, comprising approximately 4 acres, from Uriah Billings, for $4,000. (Courtesy of Peter Sarra.)

THE PRIESTS' RESIDENCE. Fr. John Flatley, who was St. John's first parish priest, lived in this residence, which stands to this day. He oversaw the congregation from 1861 until 1888, when he was transferred to Cambridge. (Courtesy of Joe DeFelice.)

THE NEW ST. JOHN'S CHURCH. Opened in 1962, this facility continues to serve the area's Catholic community, which is more than 1,400 family members strong. Father Morgan, who died at 79 in 1999, oversaw a period of great expansion of the church. For 17 years, starting in 1950, Father Morgan was a dynamic and highly respected leader. (Courtesy of Canton Public Library.)

ARCHBISHOP (LATER CARDINAL) CUSHING, c. 1961. In all likelihood, this photograph was taken in 1961 at the 100th anniversary celebration of St. John's. Shown, from left to right, are Fr. (later Msgr.) Robert E. Lee, Archbishop (later Cardinal) Cushing, and two unidentified priests. (Courtesy of Peter Sarra.)

DAVID MASCIARELLI AT HIS FIRST COMMUNION, 1938. This proud and well-attired young man celebrated his first communion at St. John's in 1938. A lifelong resident of Canton, Dave was born in 1930 in the upstairs bedroom of the house in which he currently resides on Neponset Street. Married for 48 years, he and his wife, Olive, have three children (p. 110). (Courtesy of David Masciarelli.)

Six

LANDMARKS AND
WATERWAYS

THE HISTORICAL SOCIETY, 1913. The Canton Historical Society, then, like now, consisted of many well-known town members. Pictured are Joseph A. Wattles, Arthur Brown, Harold Burt, Rachel Hewett, Helen Burt, Mildred Adams, Marilla Fitz, Marie Dans, Annie Corey, Barbara Hewett, Helen Porter, Wallace Shaw, Augustus Gill, Ralph Briggs, Richard French, Winthrop Packard, Donald McKechnie, Edwin Wentworth, George Sumner, Albert Robinson, Viola Harrington, Hobart Hewett, Philip Hewett, Mrs. Winthrop Packard, Francis Dunbar, Henri Johnson, Leonard Wolfe, Harold Burt, Mr. and Mrs. George Fred Sumner (who contributed the land where the society is located), Mr. and Mrs. H.H. Clayton, Mary Hewett, George Capen, and William Bense. (Courtesy of Canton Historical Society.)

CANTON JUNCTION, C. 1870. The name on the side of the station reads, "Canton." In 1879, the station was renamed Canton Junction. This very early photograph is taken looking toward Boston. The horse-drawn coach is from the Revere Copper Company. From 1865 until his death in 1890, the station agent, who served as an unofficial ambassador to the outside world, was Civil War veteran Jacob Silloway. (Courtesy of Canton Public Library.)

THE ORIGINAL CANTON CENTER TRAIN STATION, C. 1920. This station, built by the Boston and Providence Railroad in 1880, stood where the BankBoston–Fleet Bank is located today, by the Canton Center train station. It was demolished in 1959. (Courtesy of Canton Public Library.)

THE SPRINGDALE STATION, C. 1930. The Springdale train station was built in 1891 at a cost of $1,200, replacing the former station that was built in 1855. The station was located on Pine Street, near the waterworks (p. 96). The station closed in 1938 and was demolished two years later. In 1919, this station was used in the filming of *Anne of Green Gables*, a movie starring the then well-known movie star Mary Miles Minter. Burt Estey, a Canton mailman (p. 93), was an extra in the film. (Courtesy of Canton Public Library.)

THE CANTON JUNCTION STATION. On April 19, 1893, the Canton Junction station opened. Built by the Old Colony, it cost $12,000 to construct. The period of the 1890s was a time of great railroad expansion and modernization. It also marked a period of consolidation and transition. In a few short years, ownership was transferred from the local Boston and Providence to Old Colony to the national New York, New Haven, and Hartford Railroad. (Courtesy of Rick Saquet.)

THE CONSTRUCTION OF BLUE HILLS OBSERVATORY, C. 1885. The observatory was built in 1885 under the watchful eye of Dr. Abbott Lawrence Rotch, a professor of meteorology at Harvard University. Professor Rotch conducted state-of-the-art tests gathering various information on the winds and clouds. Harvard ran the facility until 1959, at which point the National Weather Service assumed control. (Courtesy of Mary B. Walkup.)

THE BLUE HILLS OBSERVATORY, C. 1885. The Blue Hills Observatory has recorded atmospheric temperature readings longer than any other facility in the nation. In 1980, the site was designated a National Historic landmark. In 1938, during a hurricane, wind readings were calculated in excess of 180 mph, twice as high as those recorded during the Blizzard of 1978. (Courtesy of Mary B. Walkup.)

90

Above: **AN EARLY-1900s VIEW OF THE PUBLIC LIBRARY.** (Courtesy of Canton Public Library.)
Below: **A MODERN VIEW OF THE PUBLIC LIBRARY.** (Courtesy of Mona Podgurski.) Due to the generosity of Mr and Mrs. Augustus Hemenway, who donated over $70,000 in land and construction expenses, the library was opened on July 6, 1902. Before that date, the seeds for the library were sown in 1766, when Elijah Dunbar's company lent out books. In 1801, eight gentlemen formed the Canton Social Library, which, in 1828, moved to the Canton Lyceum, located on Church and Neponset Streets. In the early 1830s, the Ladies Sewing Circle of the First Congregational Parish (Unitarian) acquired the books. Some decades later, another group formed a reading room, which was located in the Armory Building on Church Street. The armory still stands behind the Dunkin' Donuts today. The library officially came into being on June 6, 1875, when the town appropriated $500 for the purchase of books, with the stipulation that the use of the books be free to the public. In 1880, the library moved to Memorial Hall.

MEMORIAL HALL. Memorial Hall, built after a town meeting appropriated $31,000 for its construction, was dedicated on October 30, 1879. The second floor of the facility was a large auditorium, which hosted many functions. The first entertainment there was the play *Hazel Kirke*, held January 14, 1882. Today, town offices occupy the structure. (Courtesy of Joe DeFelice.)

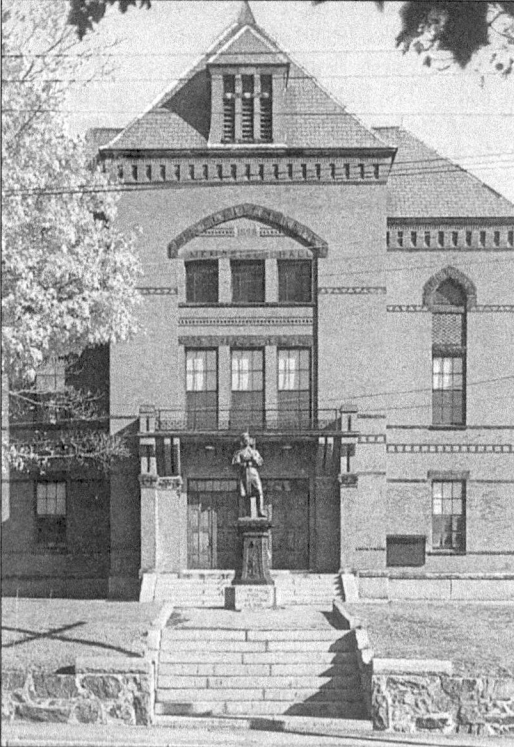

THE FRONT OF MEMORIAL HALL. The statue shown here was originally part of a drinking fountain that was placed in the vestibule of Memorial Hall in early June 1890. The fountain was a gift from Elijah A. Morse. The fountain was moved outside in September 1894. Due to vandalism, the statue was moved back inside, where it remains today. (Courtesy of Jean Galvin.)

THE STATUE IN FRONT OF MEMORIAL HALL. Starting after WWII, this statue came to the attention of pranksters. The rifle held in the arms of the solder was continually stolen. The vandalism turned ugly in 1971, when the statue itself was toppled and smashed. The pieces were gathered and stored away for five years, at which point Ernie Ciccotelli undertook the arduous task of reconstruction. Mildred Morse Allen paid for the expenses. (Courtesy of Mona Podgurski.)

THE POST OFFICE. Canton's sole post office was built in 1935. When the building was constructed, Judge Grover's house was to the left, and the Canton Diner was to the right. In 1781, it cost three shillings to mail a letter from Canton. Until the 1840s, Canton's mail was carried by stagecoach. In 1911, Canton instituted its house delivery system with three primary carriers—Frank Bomar, Herbert "Burt" Estey, and William McBride. (Courtesy of Canton Public Library.)

THE CANTON HISTORICAL SOCIETY. According to a sign in its building, the Canton Historical Society came into creation in 1873. The building itself was built in 1911. In 1997, the Bicentennial Historical Society authored *Canton Comes of Age, 1797–1997*, an excellent and worthy successor to Daniel Huntoon's tome, published in 1893. Members of the committee included highly respected local town historians Ed Lynch, Dan Keleher, Ed Bolster, Chris Brindley (curator of the Canton Historical Society), Jim Roache (president of the Canton Historical Society), and Peter Pineo. (Courtesy of Joe DeFelice.)

PONKAPOAG GRANGE NO. 231. Since 1867, Granges throughout America were established for the benefit of farmers. Canton's Grange came into existence in 1903. Initially, meeting in local Ponkapoag locations, this building was eventually erected in 1932. Located on Route 138, it is still in operation. Over the decades, it was home to fairs, dances, and town gatherings. The Grange today continues to serve the community in a variety of charitable ventures.

94

THE TRUSTEES OF THE RESERVATION. One of the nation's oldest conservation organizations operates one of Canton's great hidden gems. The Trustees of Reservations, in existence since 1891, is dedicated to acquiring and maintaining accessible land areas. There are 81 reservations throughout Massachusetts. The 82-acre site in Canton, the Bradley Reservation, is the former Cherry Hill Farm.

PEQUITSIDE. In 1809, the pastor of the First Congregational Church, William Ritchie, built this stately residence. The property was sold a few times before coming into the possession of the Draper family in 1885, where it remained until 1971, when the Town of Canton, using matching state and federal funds, purchased it for $260,000. Today the grounds, which are used for recreational purposes, are managed by the Canton Conservation Commission. Affairs are also held at the facility.

CANTON'S WORLD-FAMOUS VIADUCT. Located on Neponset Street, this fascinating structure is a marvel to the engineering world. The Viaduct, listed on the National Historic Register, was constructed between 1824 and 1836 and officially opened in 1835. Whistler's father (yes, that Whistler), Maj. Gen. George Washington Whistler, was the consulting engineer. The chief engineer was William Gibbs McNeill. The stonecutters were primarily Scottish, and the other workmen were predominantly Irish. This was the final link connecting Boston to Providence. When the viaduct was finished, the honor of the first ride across was given to Charlie, a faithful old horse who had hauled granite from the quarry in Sharon. He was pushed across on a flatcar by the workmen. (Courtesy of Canton Historical Society.)

CANTON WATERWORKS. Canton has had a strong and long-standing commitment to the purity of its water. Elijah Morse established clean drinking fountains at his estate and at the town hall. In 1888, the Canton Waterworks was established. It aided the fire department in combatting fires. (Courtesy of Mona Podgurski.)

96

FORGE POND. Not surprisingly, there was a large industrial presence on Forge Pond. In 1792, Gen. Elijah Crane built a cotton and wool factory there. The first power looms in Canton were introduced there in 1812. Twelve years later, Jonathan Messenger purchased the factory and named his mill Bolivar, after the South American hero. The town in 1840 took that name for a nearby street. (Courtesy of Joe DeFelice.)

BOLIVAR POND. From the Civil War to WWII, Bolivar Pond, also known as Ames Pond, served as a respite to those seeking relief from the heat. Unfortunately, the pond had to be closed due to pollution, most likely emanating from the town dump on nearby Pine Street. Today, the town swimming pool built on the shores of the pond provides the comfort for those attempting to escape the summer sun. (Courtesy of Joe DeFelice.)

RESERVOIR POND. This view from Pleasant Street looks toward the Wampatuck Golf Course (p. 115), which is just around the trees on the right. To this day, many people fish in the pond, except during the winter, when the pond freezes and the young and old skate on it. (Courtesy of Joe DeFelice.)

UPPER MILL POND CANT

THE UPPER MILL POND. This scenic pond is located in what had been called the Hardware section of Canton, which extended from Washington and High Streets to the Sharon-Stoughton line at Cobb's Corner. It got its name from the very successful Canton Hardware Company, established by Jonathan Robinson, in 1835.(Courtesy of Joe DeFelice.)

98

THE FALLS. The falls by Shephard's Pond is located on Washington Street, by Hagen Court, heading towards Cobbs Corner. At one time, there was a heavy industrial presence in the area. Today, it is populated by houses and apartments. (Courtesy of Joe DeFelice.)

Electric Goods Mfg. Co. Plant, Canton, Mass.

SHEPHARD'S POND. Gen. Richard Gridley once owned the iron forge and gristmill located on this pond. Gridley manufactured farm implements, among other things, until his death in 1796. In 1849, James Shephard purchased the property and established a highly successful fishing net manufacturing business. (Courtesy of Joe DeFelice.)

GLEN ECHO LAKE. This lake is another of Canton's hidden treasures. Inaccessible to the public, as private houses are built around it, the lake is located in the York Street area. Across the lake in Stoughton, a lively nightclub once stood. (Courtesy of Joe DeFelice.)

GLEN ECHO LAKE, WINTER 1936. In the 1930s, the lake area was populated only by unheated summer bungalows. Given the snow on the ground, two assumptions can easily be made. First, the obvious, it was winter. Second, no one, other than the photographer, was in the area. (Courtesy of Cynthia McDonough.)

Seven

CANTON AT WORK

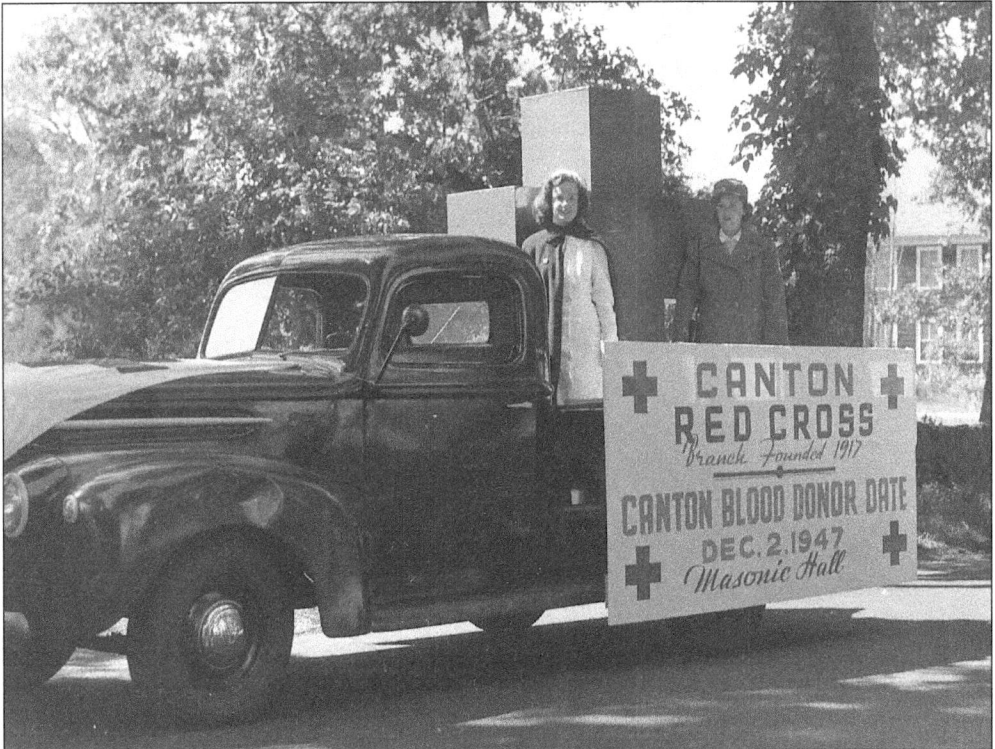

THE CANTON RED CROSS, 1947. To publicize its blood drive, this vehicle, with the assistance of some nurses, spread the word. As the sign notes, the Red Cross was established in town in 1917. (Courtesy of Canton Public Library.)

THE CANTON PUBLIC LIBRARY IN THE TOWN HALL, LATE 1800s. Canton's first official public library was located in Memorial Hall. The library continued here until the construction of the present-day library, which was built in 1902. Before the public library, books were loaned out by private individuals, usually the upper class. In the 1800s, literary societies flourished in Canton. The groups would meet, typically at someone's house, read, discuss, and swap books. The first of these societies was organized in 1766 by Elijah Dunbar. (Courtesy of Canton Public Library.)

THE CANTON INSTITUTION FOR SAVINGS. In 1835, some influential Canton residents gathered and created the 26th bank in the Commonwealth of Massachusetts, servicing the needs of Canton's population of just over 1,500 residents. The bank was located at Bent's Tavern, where today's post office stands. After several moves, the bank came to its present location in 1928. In 1988, the Canton Institution for Savings was renamed the Bank of Canton. (Courtesy of Peter Sarra.)

THE BRIGGS BROTHERS, C. 1915. This ice-cream store was one of the first such establishments in town. It was located in downtown Canton by Washington and Rockland Streets. (Courtesy of Canton Historical Society.)

AT WORK ON THE FARM, C. 1916–1928. Located on Washington Street by the Wentworth garage (p. 17), this area was a farming region. In the rear of the property was Messinger Field, where many athletic events were held. The field still exists today. (Courtesy of Peg Wentworth Morse.)

A FIRE STATION, C. LATE 1800s. In 1916, Canton left the era pictured here when the Town of Canton purchased two fire trucks. One truck was stationed at the Bolivar Street central station, which had to be enlarged to accommodate its new motorized addition. With the arrival of the new truck at Ponkapoag, the department sold its horse. (Courtesy of Mona Podgurski.)

A FIRE STATION. In 1886, this fire station was built next to the Crane School at the corner of Washington and Bolivar Streets on what today is Walgreens. It lasted nearly a century, until the last 1970s, when it was taken down. A supermarket replaced it, then Coleman's sporting goods store before Walgreens gained ownership. The station cost over $7,000 to build. It also housed a police prisoner lockup in the basement. (Courtesy of Dan Keleher.)

FIRE APPARATUS, C. EARLY 1900s. In this era, the fire department moved from a horse-drawn to a motorized unit. It also saw the hiring of full-time firefighters. Cornelius Healy and Joseph Powers were the first two full timers employed at a cost of $75 per month for each. The Crane School is in the background. One of the truck's occupants is a Mr. Cole, who died in 1954. (Courtesy of Canton Public Library.)

CALL FIREMEN FROM PONKAPOAG, 1941. Volunteer firemen still had a significant role in the 1940s. Indeed, their presence kept costs relatively stationary for many decades. The gentleman pictured on the right is James Sullivan, the owner of Crowell's in the early 1940s. (Courtesy of Canton Public Library.)

THE PLYMOUTH RUBBER COMPANY ANNUAL OUTING, 1937. Like many companies at the time, Plymouth too had an annual outing wherein the employees enjoyed a day of celebration and relaxation. Given the dress of those pictured, it was a rather formal affair. The company,

Co. Canton Mass at Fieldston Mass June 26, 1937

which was incorporated in 1898, was owned and operated by Abraham Sydeman. The business manufactured all types of rubber products. (Courtesy of Ann Galvin.)

TELEPHONE OPERATORS, 1945. Shown, from left to right, Geraldine Scully Buckley, Ann Leonard Brindley, and Blanche Bedulski work the evening shift at the switchboard of the Canton Telephone Company. The building in which they worked still exists today, as doctors' offices, on the corner of Washington and Sherman Streets, across from the library and town hall. (Courtesy of Ann Brindley.)

HOWARD JOHNSON'S, 1938. When this photograph was taken, Howard Johnson's was in its growth spurt. Founded in 1925 by Howard Dearing Johnson in Quincy, Massachusetts, the business helped establish the franchising concept. At its height, 929 franchises existed throughout the country. Today, there are 29, mainly along the East Coast. Hojo's in Canton closed its doors forever in the spring of 2000, leaving only one other restaurant in the state, in Greenfield. (Courtesy of Franchise Associates, Inc.)

KEEP OUR TOWN CLEAN, 1951. The Department of Public Works acquired this new truck in the early 1950s. Shown, from left to right, are Martin Walsh (highway foreman), Frank Carroll (selectman), Charlie Leary (selectman), William Flanagan (selectman), Tom Mullen of Morse and Mullen (a car dealership where Dunkin' Donuts is located today on Washington Street), and Herman Peters (town mechanic). (Courtesy of Charlie Tolias.)

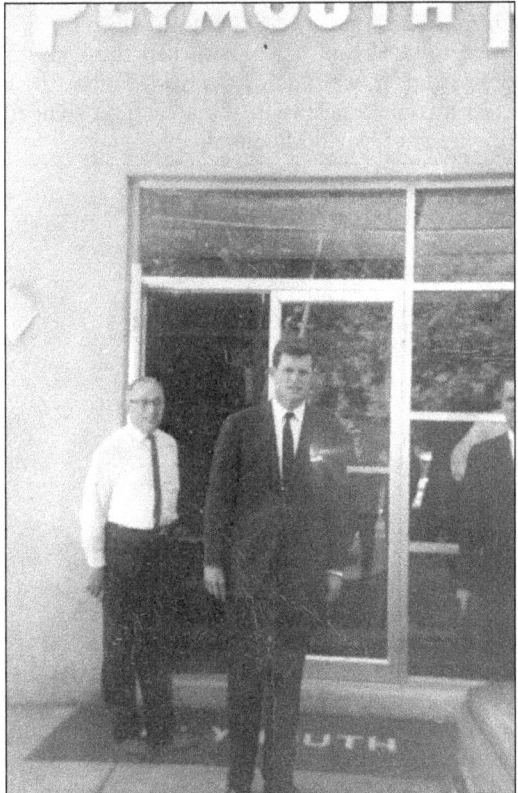

SEN. TED KENNEDY, C. 1960s. A young Ted Kennedy is seen leaving Plymouth Rubber, a worldwide manufacturer of rubber products. In the 1970s, it was the town's largest taxpayer; it also employed more than 1,000 people. To the senator's right is Jack Galvin, who ran Galvin Insurance on Washington Street. (Courtesy of Jean Galvin.)

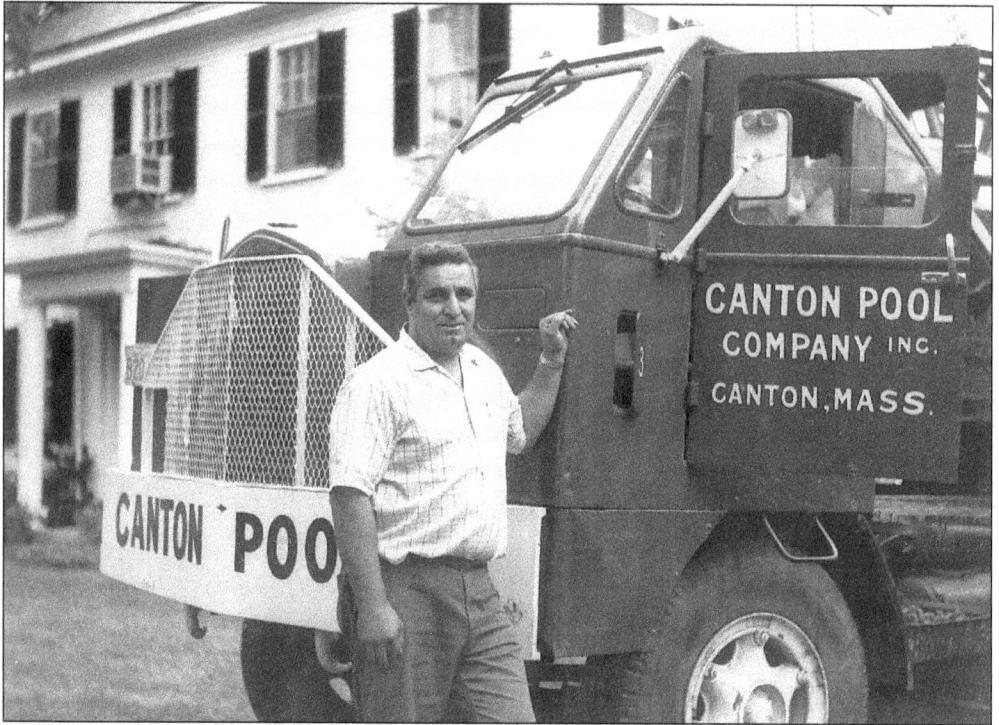

THE CANTON POOL COMPANY, C. 1960s. Approximately 40 years ago, longtime Canton resident David Masciarelli (p. 86) built a pool in his backyard. A neighbor, who liked the pool, asked Dave to build him one also. Given the high quality of the work and the likeable personality of the builder, word quickly spread. Today, the Canton Pool Company is the preeminent pool construction company in the area. The company also built the town pool on Bolivar Street. (Courtesy of David Masciarelli.)

CANTON ASSOCIATION OF INDUSTRIES (CAI) OFFICERS, 1973–1974. The CAI was formed in the early 1970s to foster a closer working relationship between the town and its many industries. Its motto is, "Serving the Community through Industry." Shown, from left to right, are Carl Whitman (secretary), Paul D. Murphy (treasurer), Lawrence F. Cedrone (president), and Henry Mann (vice president). (Courtesy of Canton Association of Industries.)

Eight

CANTON AT PLAY

THE PONKAPOAG GRANGE FLOAT, 1947. This float celebrates the contribution of Canton's farmers and its Grange (p. 94). The float was part of a parade celebrating the town's 150th anniversary. (Courtesy of Canton Public Library.)

TWO HUNTERS, 1923. Canton had its share of outdoorsmen, those who enjoyed hunting and fishing. Pictured are Nathaniel N. Wentworth (1884–1952) and Leon Storie after a successful day of hunting. (Courtesy of Peg Wentworth Morse.)

THE TOBE DEUSCHMANN BASEBALL TEAM. In the 1940s, Tobe purchased a farm located in the Ponkapoag area of Canton. Not only did the farm grow and sell corn, but it also conducted horse shows. A roadside restaurant and an electronics manufacturing business were located there. Part of the farm was taken by eminent domain for the Blue Hills Reservation. The remainder of it was sold in the 1980s. As evidenced by this picture, Tobe, pictured in the suit in the front row, also sponsored a baseball team. (Courtesy of Jean Galvin.)

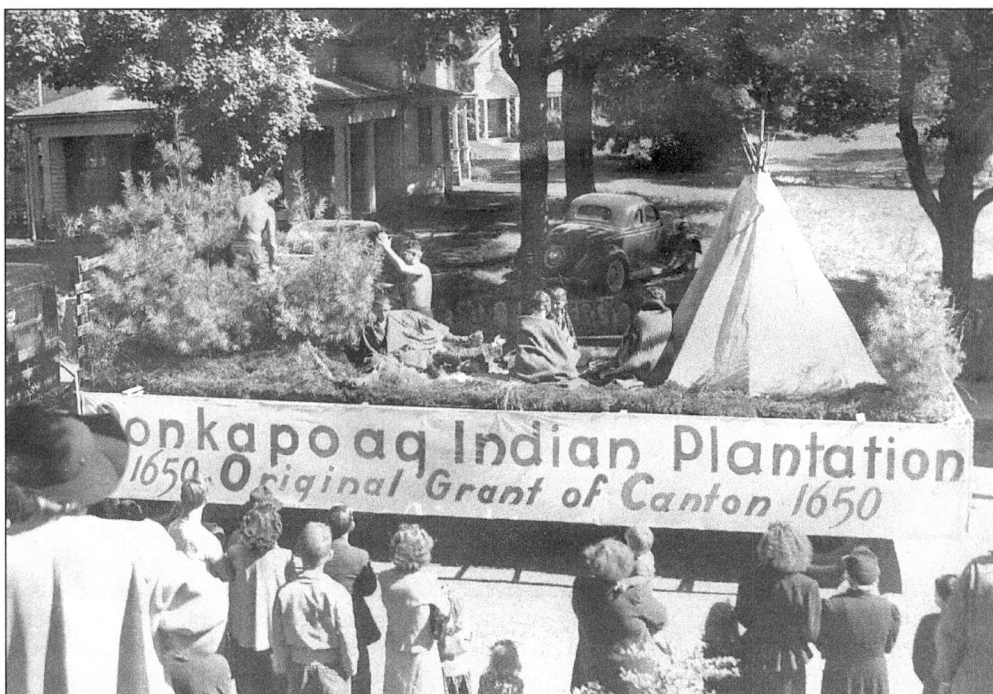

THE PARADE FLOAT COMMEMORATING THE 1650 NATIVE AMERICAN PLANTATION. In 1947, in celebration of Canton's 150th anniversary, a festive parade and party were held. This photograph shows the celebration of the legacy of the Ponkapoags, who upon settling in the Ponkapoag section of what was to become Canton, took the name. (Courtesy of Canton Public Library.)

FIVE FISHERMEN. The legacy of these five gentlemen is their love of fishing. Gene Davis and Innocenzo "Bob" Barbaglia are kneeling in front, while Mr. Porter, Joe Kessler, and Dennis Trayers back them up. The photograph was taken sometime in the late 1940s or early 1950s. (Courtesy of Jean Galvin.)

THE ORIGINAL PONKAPOAG GOLF CLUBHOUSE. In 1657, Charles Redman obtained this property from the Ponkapoag Indians and used it as farmland. Hundreds of years later, its fate was to be turned into a popular golf course, designed by noted golf course designer Donald F. Ross of Pinehurst, North Carolina. The clubhouse depicted here was destroyed by a fire. (Courtesy of Archives Department, Secretary of State William F. Galvin's office.)

CLEARING PONKAPOAG. On July 1, 1932, the clubhouse and nine holes of the golf course were opened. One year later, nine more holes were added. In 1935, another nine holes, again designed by Donald Ross, came into being. The final nine holes were added in 1959. The course is not only used for golf, but also for cross-country skiing and sledding during the winter. At any time of the year, it a lovely area to walk through. (Courtesy of Archives Department, Secretary of State William F. Galvin's office.)

WAMPATUCK GOLF COURSE. Established in 1904, this lovely club, which consists primarily of Canton residents, is rumored to be built on Native American burial grounds. Initially, it had about 32 members, a number which has now grown tenfold. In 1958, it was renovated, with much of its fill being used in the construction of the expressway. Its first hole, a par four, is thought by many to be one of the toughest starting holes in New England. (Courtesy of Canton Public Library.)

CANTON'S FIRST LITTLE LEAGUE ALL-STAR TEAM, 1952. Pictured, from left to right, are the following: (first row) team mascot Tom Southwood; (second row) Joe Healy, Joe DeFelice (p. 127), Joel Lerner, Dave Thomas, Leo McGowan, and Don Yeomans; (third row) Kim Hubbard, Bobby Trayers, Rab Russell, Paul Podgurski, Jack Ruane, Fred Darling, and Paul Callahan; (fourth row) coach Bernie Fallon, coach Dick Gardener, and manager Lonnie Southwood. (Courtesy of Joe DeFelice.)

115

TOWN CLUB FOOTBALL, C. 1954. After WWII, semiprofessional football was highly popular in this area, with Canton's Town Club being one of the very best teams in the state. In 1954, they defeated St. Paul's 21–0, Mansfield 25–0, Middleboro 14–0, Hingham 7–0, Whitman 27–13, Fairhaven 19–0, New Bedford 25–6, Hyde Park 27–0, and Randolph 44–0. They tied a powerful East Boston team 0–0. Over 9,000 people saw the championship game against South Boston, which beat our hometown heroes 14–12. With the advent of television and professional football, town club football died a quiet death in 1959. (Courtesy of Sheila Podgurski Simms.)

THE CANTON BLUEHILLSMEN. With several different names over the years, from the Baystatesmen Barbershoppers to the Canton Baystatesmen, this group started in 1959. From then to now, there have been nearly 2,000 members. Only two—Donald Wheeler (seen here on the far right) and Manny Press—have been there from the start. The group has sung on stage, television, the Esplanade, and at numerous functions. (Courtesy of Donald Wheeler.)

Nine

PAUL REVERE AND OTHER CANTON CITIZENS

OLAF HENRIKSON, RED SOX WORLD SERIES HERO, 1912. In the final game of the 1912 World Series, the Red Sox were losing to the New York Giants when, in the bottom of the seventh inning, Canton's Olaf Henrikson stepped to the plate as a pitchhitter. His key double tied the game, which the Red Sox eventually won in the bottom of the 10th inning, winning the 1912 World Series. Fifty years later, the Red Sox welcomed Olaf and his surviving teammates back (p. 128). (Courtesy of National Baseball Hall of Fame Library, Cooperstown, New York.)

PAUL REVERE. While Revere's heroics are well known, of lesser knowledge is his business acumen. He built America's first rolling copper mill in Canton, making Canton the nation's center of the copper industry. His copper was used in the hull of the USS *Constitution* as well as on Robert Fulton's ships, including the *Fulton*, the first steam-powered warship. During the War of 1812, his company produced 3 tons of copper products per week. Revere died on May 10, 1818. (Collection of the Museum of Fine Arts, Boston.)

PAUL REVERE'S HOUSE. Paul Revere referred to his home, located on the site of his copper mill, in Canton as Cantondale. It is clear from his writings that he loved his residence and the town. The original Revere Mill is still in existence and in use at the Plymouth Rubber Company on Revere Street. (Courtesy of Canton Public Library.)

REVERE COPPER YARDS. Upon the death of Paul Revere, his son Joseph Warren Revere ran the business, which merged, in 1828, with a Boston company. Numerous cannons and howitzers were made for the Union during the Civil War. Upon Joseph's death in 1867, other Revere kin managed the company, including Revere's grandson, John Revere, in 1881. After some mergers, the company relocated, leaving Canton in the very early 1900s. (Courtesy of Ann Galvin.)

REVERE MURAL IN THE CANTON POST OFFICE. Upon entering the post office, one is well advised to look at the mural above the postmaster's office. Built by those hired by the federal government during the Great Depression, it recognizes and celebrates one of Canton's greatest sons, Paul Revere.

ELIJAH MORSE. Morse was one of Canton's heavyweights. A businessman and politician, Morse served in the Massachusetts state legislature and Senate and in four sessions of Congress. He started the Rising Sun Stove Polish Company, which gained a worldwide influence. He also donated the property upon which the town hall was built. He died in 1896. (Courtesy of Ed Bolster.)

MORSE RESIDENCE. This majestic home, illustrative of a bygone era, was built in the late 1800s on land occupied today by Building B of the Canton High School. For many decades, the house was a landmark of South Canton. On the grounds stood a gazebo where a fountain provided clean water, evidence of Morse's strong commitment to establishing a healthy town water system. On July 23, 1890, this house was wired with electric light, one of the earliest houses to be so graced. (Courtesy of Canton Public Library.)

RISING SUN STOVE POLISH COMPANY. In 1864, upon his discharge from the military, where he had been captured by the Confederates in the Battle of Port Hudson (p. 29), Elijah Morse secured the formula for stove polish from a Boston chemist. Joining with his brother Albert, they created Morse Brothers, which shipped in raw materials from Ceylon to make the polish in Canton at the Rising Sun Stove Polish Works by Washington and Sherman Streets. Morse's house can be seen in the background of this picture. (Courtesy of Dan Keleher.)

EDWARD RICHARDS MAYO, c. 1870s. The Mayo house on Elm Street had been in possession of the Mayo family for well over a century. Even after its sale, it has had but a few owners in its 150-year existence. A nearby neighbor was Commodore Downes, a great naval hero who died in 1854. (Courtesy of Dr. John Crowe.)

121

THOMAS BAILEY ALDRICH. Aldrich was a famous author and good friend of Mark Twain. His book *The Story of a Bad Boy*, published in 1870, served as inspiration for Tom Sawyer (1876) and Huck Finn (1880). Another close Aldridge friend was Edwin Booth, brother of John Wilkes Booth. Booth introduced Aldridge to his future wife, Lillian Woodman. Aldrich in turn later wrote the epitaph appearing on Booth's headstone. (Courtesy of Anthony Mitchell Sammarco.)

THE PASADENA CLUB, C. 1900. These prosperous first-generation Canton men pose in their Sunday best outside of Charlie Grimes's stable, which was located across from St. John's Church on Washington Street. They are, from left to right, as follows: (sitting) unidentified, unidentified, Charlie Riley, unidentified, Eddie Clancy, and Phil Danahy; (standing) Charlie Grimes, Jim Lyod, Kathleen McKenna's father, Jim Murphy, Mat Galligan, John Riley, and James Grimes. (Courtesy of Edward D. Galvin.)

DOROTHY WHIPPLE McKEE AS A BABY, C. LATE 1890S. Dorothy, who was born in 1897, is pictured with her parents, Andrew J. and Lucy S. McKee in North Stoughton. The horse's name was Billy. Dorothy (p. 80) moved to Canton after her marriage to Nathaniel Newcomb Wentworth (p. 112). (Courtesy of Peg Wentworth Morse.)

DOROTHY McKEE SENDING HER SON OFF TO WWII. Nathaniel Newcomb Wentworth Jr. (pp. 33, 125) served his nation with distinction. As a commanding officer, 83rd Division, 331st Infantry Regiment, Company M, he saw action in the Normandy campaign in the vicinity of Carentan and Periers, France. (Courtesy of Peg Wentworth Morse.)

DAN LYONS, C. LATE 1800S. The occasion for the attire of this nattily dressed young man is lost to the ages. Perhaps, it was a wedding or engagement picture. What is known is that he married Clara Chandler, a twin, the great aunt of Canton resident Jean Galvin. (Courtesy of Jean Galvin.)

MRS. CHANDLER, JEAN GALVIN'S MOTHER. Hats were of great stylish splendor for a great many decades. Whether it was off to a wedding or simply time to get a new bonnet for Easter, a trip to the local store was in order. (Courtesy of Jean Galvin.)

NATHANIEL N. WENTWORTH JR., AGE FIVE, 1922. Nathaniel was born in 1917 and died in 1992. He had a long and distinguished career as a civil engineer, working on some of the most notable construction projects in the commonwealth. He was also a significant civic leader. Just a few of his many contributions include his helping establish the Blue Hills Regional High School, chair of the planning board, founding chair of the Canton Housing Authority and chair, president, and vice president over the years at the Canton Cooperative Bank. (Courtesy of Peg Wentworth Morse.)

THE PARRISH BROTHERS, SPRING 1933. Stan Parrish, a resident of Canton, co-owned and operated the well-known Crescent Ridge Farm, located in the neighboring town of Sharon. Stan, pictured on the right, was born in 1931, to Malby and Mildred Parrish, who purchased the farm in 1932. The Parrishes had two other boys, Paul (left), an architect who died in the late 1960s and Bob (middle), who ran the dairy with Stan. Both Stan and Bob are now retired. (Courtesy of the Parrish family.)

DANIEL HUNTOON, CANTON'S FOREMOST HISTORIAN. Daniel T.V. Huntoon was born in Canton on September 4, 1842. He was the son of Rev. Benjamin and Lydia (Baker) Huntoon. He passed away on a Wednesday afternoon on December 15, 1886. Daniel took an active part in Canton's development, serving on the school committee, as superintendent of Canton's schools, and as a moderator at town meetings. He was a businessman and historian, having written the 650-plus page *History of Canton, Massachusetts* in 1893. (Courtesy of Canton Public Library.)

ED BOLSTER, 1957. A longtime Canton historian and activist, Ed was born in 1915. He was the president of the Canton Historical Society for 21 years. A part-time actor, his credits go all the back to 1930, when he starred as the Reverend Mr. Wilson in a play held at the Crane School graduation exercises. He also did summer stock in Maine as well as in Boston. He carries an unsurpassed knowledge of the town. (Courtesy of Ed Bolster.)

JOE DEFELICE, KOREA, 1965. A true lover of Canton, Joe has contributed much to the town, serving on numerous committees and boards (p. 76) over the years. A superb athlete throughout his life (p. 115), he is shown in his I Corps, 8th Army baseball uniform, one of many championship teams, both military and civilian, on which he played. A longtime columnist for the *Canton Journal*, he keeps his readers abreast of the latest town news. (Courtesy of Joe DeFelice.)

BICENTENNIAL COMMITTEE, 1997. The Bicentennial Committee was the motor that drove Canton's 200th anniversary celebration in 1997. Shown, from left to right, are the following: (first row) Ada Goodrich, Norma Gaynor, and Maureen Dickie; (second row) Lee Thompson, Sue Reddington, and Linda Cammarata; (third row) Clyde Pushard, Dan Keleher, Bill Armando, Ed Lynch, Al D'Attanasio, and Joe Uliano; (fourth row) Dick Staiti, and Cab Devoll. Dan Keleher and Ed Lynch (along with Ed Bolster and Peter Sarra) are the senior class of Canton's most highly regarded town historians. (Courtesy of Al D'Attanasio.)

BEAUTIFICATION AWARD TO SARRA BROTHERS, C. 1980S. Shown, from left to right, are Tony Andreotti (selectman), Peter Sarra, Frank Sarra, Dan Flood, Lee Gibson, Dick Staiti (selectman), and Ed Lynch (selectman). Like Ed Lynch, Peter Sarra has a remarkable knowledge of Canton. Born in the house in which he has lived his entire life, he has made many contributions to the town. He is known to his friends, business associates, and old school chums by different names—Peter, Richie, or Sam. (Courtesy of Peter Sarra.)

FIFTIETH ANNIVERSARY OF THE 1912 RED SOX WORLD SERIES CHAMPIONS, 1962. In 1962, the Red Sox welcomed nine surviving members of their 1912 World Series team. From left to right, they are Bill Carrigan, Steve Yerkes, Smokey Joe Wood, Larry Gardner, Duffy Lewis, "Canton's Own" Olaf Henrikson (p. 117), Ray Collins (in wheelchair), Hugh Bedient, Harry Hooper, Dick O'Connell (representing Red Sox management), and Joe McKenney (representing the president of the American League, Joe Cronin). (Courtesy of Marie Leary.)

www.ingramcontent.com/pod-product-compliance
Lightning Source LLC
Chambersburg PA
CBHW050923150426
42812CB00051B/1997